Why The Star Wars Prequels Sucked and Why It Matters

Delano José Lopez

Dedication

Respectfully dedicated to the George Lucas of 1977

Acknowledgments

Special thanks to my older brother Dominic, not only for many years of discussion of fantasy, science fiction, art, drama and literature, but also, for telling my parents when I was seven that I wouldn't be scared by the cantina aliens, and thus it was okay for me to go see *Star Wars*.

ISBN 978-1-300-45676-6

Table of Contents

Introduction

The premiere of Star Wars Episode 1: *The Phantom Menace* in 1999 was arguably the most anticipated event in modern popular culture. Devoted fans camped out months in advance, theaters staged special midnight showings, and millions turned out for its opening- many in elaborate home made costumes of characters from the original trilogy. Equally monumental was the disappointment with the film, especially among some of Star Wars' most devoted fans.

Filmmaker Kevin Smith is perhaps as big a fan of the original trilogy as exists. Most of his films contain at least some reference to Star Wars. For example, his break-out independent film, *Clerks,*(1994) contains a discussion of the ethics of destroying the incomplete Death Star in *Return of the Jedi* while killing the civilian construction workers on board. Yet in one episode of his animated television show also named *Clerks,* (2000) one of the protagonists swears Lucas in as a witness at a trial, and then browbeats him with the numerous contradictions and inconsistencies of *The Phantom Menace,* and demands his money back. The cartoon Lucas finally concedes that the film was hastily written over a weekend, and refunds the ticket price.

Actor and director Seth Green, in an episode of his television show *Robot Chicken* parodied the climactic scene from *The Empire Strikes Back* in which Darth Vader reveals to Luke Skywalker that he is Luke's father. In Green's parody, Vader follows this with a series of even more implausible revelations from the prequels, such as the Midichlorians, and Vader constructing C-3PO. Luke finally walks out on Vader, saying that Vader (and perhaps by extension, George Lucas) is not taking this seriously.

Perhaps most graphic in expressing his disappointment, stand-up comedian Brian Posehn equated the experience of watching the prequels to being molested by a favorite uncle. Fellow comedian Patton Oswalt asserts that if he had a time machine he would go back in time and murder George Lucas with a shovel before he could make the prequels.

Some fans were so disappointed that they felt the need to re-edit the film. The "Phantom Edit", "The Phantom Re-Edit" and others tried to salvage the film by editing out or modifying its most obvious flaws, chief of which was Jar-Jar Binks,-we'll return to him later.

But these were merely exercises in turd-polishing, for the flaws of the *Phantom Menace* and the other prequels (*Attack of the Clones* and *Revenge of the Sith)* were so deep as to be beyond salvage. It was not merely the *presence* of some annoying characters that was wrong with the film, but it was profound *absences* that doomed it to failure. It is these absences, as well as the other flaws, that this work will examine at length.

This colossal three-time failure of an otherwise brilliant film maker would be worthy of study on its own. Yet, I would argue the importance of this extends beyond merely the realm of film studies. Pop culture is the repository of the mythology of the modern age, and there is little within it as iconic as the Star Wars mythos. These pop culture mythologies both reflect and shape the ethics and morality of our society. Indeed, Star Wars is a series of grand morality tales, writ on an epic scale. It is the failure of the prequels to live up to the ethical ideals of the original trilogy that is ultimately responsible for the artistic failure of the films, the sense of violation by the devotees, and the need to examine this failing in depth.

This work will examine the prequels by first looking at the most obvious and superficial problems, and then work toward ever deeper and more significant problems, including a comparison with the original trilogy, identification of the key missing element, and a final argument for the cultural, political and moral importance of these failings.

A note on terminology

The numbering and chronology of the Star Wars films can be confusing. Referring to the "first" films is unclear, as it could refer to either the first in order of release, or the first in terms of plot. The original film, first simply titled *Star Wars* was released in 1977. This film was later subtitled *A New Hope* and given the designation Episode 4, suggesting the three prequels yet to come. The next two films, *The Empire Strikes Back* (Episode 5) and *Return of the Jedi* (Episode 6) were released in 1980 and 1983, respectively. They were numbered episodes 4-6, because of their position in the internal chronology of the films, not because of the order in which they were released. The next three films, *The Phantom Menace, Attack of the Clones,* and *The Revenge of the Sith,* are episodes 1 through 3, released in 1999, 2002, and 2005. These ones are set approximately twenty years before the events of episodes 4-6. To clarify my terms, I will refer to episodes 4-6 as the "original" films or trilogy, and episodes 1-3 as the "prequels."

I should also note here that while the Star Wars films have inspired hundreds of licensed video games, books, comics, television specials and series, (what the fan community refers to as the "Extended Universe") my critique will limit itself to only the six theatrically released films.

Synopsis

For the casual reader, a synopsis of the plot of the prequel trilogy will be provided. (Even many devoted fans of the original trilogy may need a refresher, as many, like I, may have avoided the prequels after an initial viewing because of their disappointing nature. Those who are more familiar with the plot and characters of the prequels may wish to skip ahead to "What Went Wrong.")

This trilogy follows the development of Anakin Skywalker from young slave boy, to Jedi *padwan* (or apprentice) to Sith apprentice and finally, Sith Lord Darth Vader. Simultaneously, it chronicles the political manipulations of Senator Palpatine, who is secretly the Sith Lord Darth Sidious, to replace the Republic with the Galactic Empire, and have himself named Emperor. Because both of these developments are already established in the original trilogy, the audience already knows their outcomes, and, like the characters in the film, must watch pre-ordained events unfold.

Phantom Menace

The first film of the prequels, *The Phantom Menace*, begins as two Jedi knights, Qui-Gon Jinn and his apprentice, Obi-Wan Kenobi, are dispatched by the Galactic Chancelor Valorum to the planet Naboo, to negotiate an end to a blockade of the planet by the Trade Federation. The Jedi Knights are spiritual warrior monks, who seem to hold a quasi-governmental position as diplomats and law enforcement officers. They derive supernatural powers from their mastery of "The Force." (The Sith are the Jedi's opposite number – followers of the Dark Side of the Force.)

The Trade Federation is headed by an alien race called the Neimoidians. However, they have been manipulated into their actions by Darth Sidious, a Sith Lord, as part of his plan to create a threat to the Republic that will allow him to take power. When confronted over the blockade by the Jedi, the Neimodians attack the Jedi with their battle droids. The Jedi flee from the droids, during which they encounter and join up with Jar-Jar Binks, a Gungan, a member of a primitive race indigenous to the oceans of Naboo. With Jar-Jar's help, they travel to the capital of

Naboo where they meet the ruler of the planet, Queen Amidala.

The Trade Federation blockade becomes a full blown invasion, and the Queen and the Jedi flee Naboo to seek help from the Galactic Senate on the capital planet Coruscant. However, during their flight the ship is damaged, and they must land on Tatooine. There they meet the young slave boy Anakin Skywalker, and must sponsor him in a pod race in order to earn the money to repair their ship. Qui-Gon Jinn learns that Anakin is strong in the Force and decides to free him from Watto, his master, and take him to Corsucant to train him as a Jedi. During the time on Tatooine, Queen Amidala masquerades as her own handmaiden Padme.

After successfully repairing their ship, the party leaves for Coruscant. While leaving the planet, they are attacked , inconclusively, by Darth Maul, Darth Sidious' apprentice. On Coruscant, Amidala is manipulated by Senator Palpatine to call for a vote of no confidence in the Chancelor, allowing Palpatine to take his place. Meanwhile, Obi-wan and Qui-Gon present Anakin to the Jedi Council for training, but the Council refuses, citing his age, fear and anger.

The Jedi, Amidala, et. al. return to Naboo, where they lead an army of Gungans against the Droid army of the Trade Federation. During this battle, Anakin demonstrates his flying skills and destroys the central computer that controls the Droids. There is also a battle between Darth Maul, and the two Jedi, in which Darth Maul kills Qui-Gon Jinn, (in an echo of the death of Ben Kenobi at the end of a New Hope) and Obi-Wan in turn kills Darth Maul.

The dying Qui-Gon instructs Obi-Wan to teach Anakin, which Yoda reluctantly allows.

The Attack of the Clones

Set ten years after the action of the first film, the plot of *Attack of the Clones* further advances the meta-plot of the trilogy, (already known to those who have followed the original films) - the destruction of the old republic and the rise of Senator Palpatine as Emperor and the transformation of Anakin into Darth Vader.

A separatist movement led by a former Jedi, Count Dooku, is seeking independence from the Republic. Queen Amidala now represents Naboo in the Galactic Senate, on the capital planet of Coruscant. An attempt on her life, via a bomb on her ship, narrowly fails. In response to this the Jedi assign Anakin and Obi-wan to protect her. The two thwart an assassin's second attempt on her life, and Obi-wan is sent to investigate the attempted assassinations.

In the course of his investigation Kenobi discovers on the planet Kamino an army of clones that was secretly ordered to be constructed for the Jedi decades ago, without the Council's knowledge, by a now long dead Jedi. The council decides to use these clones to fight the droid army of the Separatists.

Meanwhile, as Anakin is guarding Padme, the two fall in love. Anakin receives a vision that his mother is in danger, and travels to Tatooine to save her.

He discovers that she has been captured by the indigenous Sand People. He finds her dying, and takes out his revenge on the Sand People, killing the entire encampment, including women and children. Racked with grief, he tells Padme that he has killed them all, including children.

Obi-Wan follows the bounty hunter Jango Fett, who is both the genetic donor for the clone army, and the suspected would-be assassin of Padme, to the planet Geonosis. Obi-wan, Anakin and Padme reunite there, where the Separatist leader Count Dooku is assembling a droid army. The three attempt to infiltrate the droid factory, are captured, and are placed in a a Roman Colosseum-style arena, to be thrown to the space-lions. They escape with the help of several dozen Jedi, and the arriving clone army, led by Yoda. There is a large chaotic battle between the Separatist's droids and the Republic's clones. Yoda , Obi-Wan and Anakin battle Dooku with lightsabers. Dooku manages to escape, after cutting off Anakin's arm.

The clone wars have officially begun, so says Yoda, ("Begun these Clone Wars have.") and Palpatine gets the Senate to accept the clones as the Republic's Army. The film ends with a secret marriage between Amidala and Anakin, after he has had a cybernetic hand added. This both calls back to and foreshadows the ending of the *Empire Strikes Back*, in which Luke has had his wrist cut off by Vader, and replaced with a cybernetic one.

The Revenge of the Sith

The last of the prequels begins mid battle. The Republic and the Jedi are still fighting the Separatists and their Droid army, three years after the events of the previous film. Chancellor Palpatine has been captured by Count Dooku and General Grievous, the cybernetic commander of the droids. This is, of course, part of Palpatine's Machiaveliean schemes, and when Obi-Wan and Anakin arrive to rescue Palapatine, he uses the opportunity to goad Anakin into killing Dooku, (while Obi-Wan is conveniently unconscious) thus bringing him closer to the Dark Side.

After rescuing the Chancellor, Anakin is assigned as his bodyguard. Meanwhile, Padme reveals to Anakin that she is pregnant. However, Anakin has a vision of Padme dying in childbirth, similar to a vision he had of his mother before she died. Palpatine manipulates Anakin's fear of Padme's death by telling Anakin that the Sith had the secrets of life, including being able to create life and prevent death. Meanwhile, the Jedi Council, suspicious of Palpatine has asked Anakin to spy on Palpatine for them, while Palapatine has asked the same of him vis a vis the Jedi Council.

Obi-Wan travels to the planet Utapau, cuurently in the hands of the Separtists. There he battles and defeats the Droid leader General Grievous.

Palpatine tells Anakin that he is the Sith Lord Darth Sidious. Anakin then tells the Jedi Council, who sends Jedi Master Mace Windu to confront Plapatine. During this confrontation, Sidious tells Anakin that if he allows Windu to kill him, that he will never learn the Sith secrets of prolonging life, and thus, Padme is doomed to die. Anakin then kills Windu, and then follows Palpatine's instructions to kill the remaining Jedi, including the children being trained in the Jedi Temple.

Simultaneously, Palpatine triggers a secret order – Order 66 – to the clone army to kill all of the Jedi who are serving with them as they battle in the Clone Wars. All are slain save Obi-wan and Yoda.
Yoda confronts the Emperor in a lightsaber duel that ends in a draw, with Yoda retreating to his self imposed exile on Dagobah.

Obi-wan rushes to confront Anakin by smuggling himself aboard a shuttle craft that Amidala is taking to rendezvous with Anakin on the planet Mustafar. Amidala attempts to convert Anakin back to the Light Side of the Force, but when he spies Obi-wan emerging from the shuttle, he thinks Padme has betrayed him and attempts to strangle her. Obi Wan and Anakin engage in an epic lightsaber duel, that ends with Obi Wan cutting off Anakin's arms and legs, and leaving him to burn to death in molten lava.

However, the Emperor rescues Anakin, encases him in the now familiar black armor, and christens him "Darth Vader." Meanwhile, Padme dies from complications of giving birth to Vader's children, though she names them Luke and Leia before she dies. Thus all the pieces are set for Episode Four.

What Went Wrong

Here begins the critique of the flaws of the

films, roughly arranged in order from least to most serious. That will be followed with an analysis of why the originals were so good, and a comparison between the two. Finally the work will conclude with a discussion of the ethical and political ramifications of the films and their flaws.

The Many Minor Flaws

First, Jar-Jar

Jar-Jar Binks was by far the most annoying new character introduced in *Phantom Menace*. He speaks in a blend of Elmo's childish falsetto and a Carribean patois. Jar-Jar's function is clearly that of comic relief, but he is so incessant that rather than providing "relief" in an otherwise serious film, the *Phantom Menace* becomes a comedy, but an unfunny one. His clownishness was all the more troublesome in that his obsequiousness to the film's white protagonists and his accent were reminiscent of the "Stepin Fetchit"-style characters of minstrel shows and early film.

Many elements of the classic movies and movie serials of Lucas's youth appear in the Star Wars films, such as the "wipes"- transitions from one scene to another- the use of literal cliffhangers, etc. One less pleasant hold-over from that era is that of the obsequious non-white servant, especially who, for little discernible reason falls into immediate devoted service to the white protagonists. The Lone Ranger's Tonto and the Green Hornet's Kato (both initially created for radio by the same man, Fran Striker) are two of the best known examples of the non-white subservient sidekick. This became such an unthinking cliché of films of the forties that it was parodied in Carl Reiner's *Dead Men Don't Wear Plaid.* In that film, the Peruvian police chief goes so far as to iron the American protagonist's pajamas.

In the first trilogy, the role of loyal servant and comic relief is primarily played by the two droids, C-3PO and R2-D2. This makes sense, as they are robots, beings intentionally created for servitude and programmed to obey their masters, unlike the sentient Gungan Jar-Jar Binks, who presumably has free will. Further isolating the droids from the colonial connotations of their service is the fact that C-3PO speaks with a proper British accent, and is more reminiscent of a butler than a slave. (Unfortunately, slavery is a recurring theme in the prequels which we will return to it at greater length later.) C-3PO, while somewhat cowardly and clumsy, is also rightly proud of his skills as a protocol droid and his fluency in "over six million forms of communication."

Jar-Jar has no such redeeming qualities, and his similarity to a shuffling, minstrel show performer was painful to watch. *Mad TV* satirized Jar-Jar's minstrelsy by having Lucas introducing his Aunt Jar-Jarmima, complete with red checkered kerchief on her head, and, referencing *Gone With The Wind,* shouts of "Lordy, I don't know nothin' 'bout no Jedis."

Aaron McGruder parodied this in his *Boondocks* comic strip, first by having Jar-Jar appear as a shuffling “stepin fetchit,” then in later strips by having Jar-Jar achieve some race consciousness, appearing in a black beret, changing his name, and acting like a militant of the seventies black power movement. (This was also the trajectory followed in real life by actor Lincoln Perry, the original Stepin Fetchit, who converted to Islam in the Sixties and was active in the civil rights movement.)

Lucas may have responded to criticism of the character by minimizing his appearance in the two subsequent films,and generally portraying him with more dignity. Despite being elevated to the Galactic Senate in *Attack of the Clones,* he remains a fool, as he is easily manipulated into nominating Senator Palpatine for chancellor, a key step toward the latter's rise to Emperor.

Further, the planet of Naboo is divided between between the Gungans and the Nabooians. The former, Jar-Jar's people, are more culturally and technologically primitive and live in underwater cities, while the Nabooians, identical to the rest of the humans throughout the Galaxy, live on the surface with more elaborate and technologically advanced cities. While the history of the planet is never explained, this clearly seems to be a case of the Nabooians as “benevolent” colonizers, and the Gungans as the colonized, who have been marginalized and pushed to the fringes of their own planet. Yet the Gungans as a whole are willing to follow Jar-Jar's subservient lead and assist the Nabooians in fighting the trade federation, even though, as the Gangans have no spacecraft, it seems that the interstellar trade embargo is aimed not at them, but their colonizers. While there are historical precedents for this level of collaboration with one's colonists- the Gurkha regiments of India fighting the Germans for the British, the Code Talkers fighting the Japanese for the Americans,- it is an oddly un-heroic exploitation of the sub-altern for our heroes to be engaged in.

Moreover, Jar-Jar is not the only character in the prequels to have racist overtones. Watto, the alien slave owner of Anakin and his mother, Shmi, had a large, almost prehensile nose, a stubbly beard, and spoke with an accent that could be either Eastern European or Middle Eastern. He was also so singly focused on money as to be immune to Jedi mind tricks. He was viewed by many as an anti-semitic stereotype, some seeing him as Jewish, others as an Arab.

The lead alien race of the trade federation, the Neimodians, were also criticized as a racist Asian stereotype. They speak with an Asian accent, have slanted alien eyes, are aggressive, duplicitous traders, and dress in elaborate, ornate robes. This is reminiscent both of economic fears of Japan, (in the Eighties) and China (in the Nineties) as well as the yellow menace stereotype of the pulp fiction era, such as in Sax Rohmer's *Dr. Fu Manchu* stories.

The Pod Race

The conflict and obstacles in *The Phantom Menace* are rather insipid. To serve the overarching plot of the trilogy, it is necessary to introduce Anakin, and have him taken from his home to study with the Jedi. Yet, since most of this first movie is merely an introduction to plot elements that will be further developed later, the major obstacle to the protagonists is that they are stranded on Tatooine and need to purchase a replacement part for their spaceship. In order to make this fairly trivial task difficult for the Jedi, Watto, the junk dealer who has the part, (and who also owns Anakin and his mother) is immune to the mind control powers of the Force.

This is one of the many instances in the prequels where the Force is downgraded from a mystic, communing-with-the-God-head-like power of the entire universe, as it is in the original three movies, to something merely akin to psychic powers and parlor tricks. True, it has been established in the original trilogy that the Force's mind control power only works on the "weak-minded," and the crime lord Jabba the Hutt is able to resist them, but it cheapens the Force to have a two bit-junk dealer able to resist a powerful Jedi.

The junk dealer will also not take Republic credits, and so because of these contrivances, the Jedi have to engage in gambling to earn the money to repair the ship. Rather than defeating great evil and defending the innocent, much of the film is wasted on what is essentially the Jedi's heroic struggle to fix their car. This contrivance leads to the Pod-race sequence, in which Anakin enters a form of space chariot racing, reminiscent of the great "sandal operas" of cinema, such as Ben Hur. Indeed, the design of the "pods" has the pilot seated behind and attached by tethers to two forward engines, as a chariot would be drawn by two horses.

One of the many dramatic flaws of the prequels is that by trivializing its villains and struggles, it trivializes its heroes. By the end of the pod race, at an equivalent point in *A New Hope*, an entire planet has been destroyed, people have been strangled to death, our heroine has been tortured, and the hero has seen the charred corpses of his adoptive parents. In comparison, the heroes of Phantom Menace have had to deal with the equivalent of a blow-out on the highway. Sure, the Trade Federation has threatened the residents of Naboo, but they are cartoonish, not fearsome, and any hardship suffered by the Nabooians occurs well off screen. There is hardly any menace in this film at all.

This is a problem that will continue throughout the prequels, of a dilution of the struggles, a weakening of the moral choices that can be made and a negation of the importance of the characters' actions.

C-3PO and R2D2

Another nonsensical element in Phantom Menace is in the origin of C-3PO. Lucas had long established that the only characters which would be present in all nine Star Wars films (the original trilogy, plus three prequels and three, as yet unmade, sequels) would be the two droids, R2-D2 and C-3PO. It has been further suggested that the films could be thought of as being told from the droids' point of view. This later point could not be literally true, as many scenes take place with neither droid present. However, they remain important, if secondary, characters throughout the first trilogy.

Much has been made of the fact that these two characters were based on peasant characters in the Akira Kurasawa film *The Hidden Fortress* (1958) though the similarity to the Kurasawa characters is slight. They are devoted servants, and somewhat detached observers of the action. R2 is a bit of a trickster, and also performs the role of a thief in this band of adventurers, performing the electronic equivalent of lock picking. They also perform comic relief, having a rough physical resemblance to classic comedy teams like Abbot and Costello or Laurel and Hardy. But the two droids are separated from each other for most of the prequels, thus having little chance to function together as a comedy team.

C-3PO's humor arises from his exaggerated sense of dignity and the undignified positions into which he is thrown. This is a result of his function, for, as he repeats throughout the original trilogy, he is an etiquette and protocol droid, well versed in over six million forms of communication.

It made perfect sense for C-3PO, the etiquette and protocol droid, to be present in the entourage of Princess Leia in a *New Hope*, as she is a senator and diplomat. It makes no sense, however, for him to be introduced in the *Phantom Menace* as having been built from scrap by the young Anakin. There are plenty of diplomats and politicians in *Phantom Menace* who would have need of such a droid, serving to introduce the character to the prequels. Why would a nine year old slave boy have the interest or the means to build a protocol droid? If it were necessary for Anakin to have built any droid, R2-D2 would have made more sense, as R2 units are used by pilots, and Anakin has a boy's interest in flying and racing. He doesn't seem to have any interest in etiquette, and as Uncle Owen says in a *New Hope*, there is no use for a protocol droid among the farmers of Tatooine. This is yet another example of what appears to be a lack of serious thought put into the story by Lucas.

Light Sabers

There is great mythic power attached to swords in Western culture. Acquiring a sword and learning to wield it are important steps on the hero's journey, and much could be made of the sword as symbol of the Nietzchean (not to mention Freudian) will to power. Excalibur is the archetypal example of this. When Luke receives his father's lightsaber from Ben in *A New Hope,* he is being inducted into the ranks of heroes, much as Arthur is by drawing Excalibur from the Stone, or receiving it from the Lady of the Lake. Fantasy fiction writers are aware of the importance of swords, often naming them, such as Gandolf's Glamdring or Elric of Melnibone's Stormbringer, thus making them legendary. (Samuel L. Jackson was likely aware of the importance of the unique sword, as he requested that the lightsaber for his character, Mace Windu, have a purple blade, which no other lightsaber has.)

Such swords have power, and danger, and thus should be used carefully. Ben tells Luke that a light saber is “from a more civilized age.”, thus it is a symbol of chivalry and nobility. From a dramatic perspective, such weapons should also be used rarely, as to avoid diluting their power, and cheapening their importance. Indeed, Lucas uses the lightsaber sparingly in the original trilogy. We only see four in total in the three movies, Luke's original, given to him by Ben and once owned by Anakin, Ben's, Darth Vader's, and Luke's replacement saber, after he loses his original in *The Empire Strikes Back.* Moreover, these are used frugally, but to dramatic effect every time they appear. There are only ten total scenes in which lightsabers are turned on in the three original movies, and we don't see a full-blown duel until the end of the second film. Drawing the lightsaber is important, and there is often a warning before it is drawn. On Mos Eisley, and again on Jabba's Sail Barge, Ben and Luke try to resolve conflicts without violence, before unsheathing their blades. Further emphasizing the chivalric nature of these knights, Luke's sword is carried for him to the Sail Barge battle by his “squire,” RD-D2.

The three lightsaber duels at the end of each of the three original films are crucial to the plot and the development of Luke as a character. Moreover, they are exciting in that we are uncertain of their outcome.

In fact, the heroes, Ben and Luke, lose the first two to Vader.

In contrast, we already know the outcome of most of the duels in the prequels, as we know that Yoda, Ben, Anakin and the Emperor will all survive to the time setting of the original films. Thus, there is little suspense or excitement to any of the many duels involving these characters.

In the prequels, there are too many lightsabers, and too many duels. Thus the weapons lose their gravitas, and the fights lose their drama. In one duel alone, (between Ben and General Grevious,) there are more lightsabers (five) than appeared in all three of the original movies. The total number of lightsabers is in the dozens, (in a cameo appearance, each member of N'sync gets one), they are ever present, and there are at least six major, but inconsequential, duels. They have become a far too common tool. It wasn't until *Return of the Jedi* that Luke first used the light saber to defend against blasters, and he only once uses this offensively, to deflect a blast black to his target.

In the prequels, the lightsaber is used to block blasts constantly, and so frequently in the offensive fashion, that it raises the question as to why the Jedi don't just carry their own blasters. Surely the lightsaber, praised by Kenobi in *A New Hope* as not as "clumsy or random" as a blaster, is not less clumsy when deflecting blaster rays? More importantly, constantly reflecting blasts back on the attacker makes the lightsaber seem gimicky. Most importantly, as familiarity breeds contempt, the overuse of the lightsaber in the prequels reduces its iconic significance.

There is a lightsaber duel at the end of *Phantom Menace* between Qui-Gon Jinn and Darth Maul that seems to serve no other dramatic purpose than having a lightsaber duel. It does nothing to advance the plot, as both characters are disposable- Qui Gon's role as teacher is taken over by Kenobi in the later film, and Darth Maul's position as apprentice Sith is taken by Count Dooku. The fight, no matter which way it would turn out, does not advance Darth Sideous' plans either. It seems that the only reason for this battle is because the fans would expect a lightsaber duel.

Queen Amidala is no Princess Leia

Queen Amidala is a poor comparison to Princess Leia. In *A New Hope*, Princess Leia was a smart, strong willed and powerful female hero. In fact, much of the humor of the first film comes from Leia turning an old fantasy cliché on its head. The heroes set out to rescue the princess from the castle of the evil wizard. Rather than swooning in gratitude, Leia insults the heroes (and their space ship,) and aggressively takes a hand in her own rescue. She is a leader of a rebellion, and stands up to Darth Vader and Grand Moff Tarken.

She is not without flaws, however,as she is a bit racist toward Chewbacca, referring to him as a “walking carpet” and saying she'd rather kiss a Wookie than Han, implying that there is something unappealing about Wookies. Perhaps her aristocratic upbringing explains this. By the end of the films, she does come to exhibit real fondness for Chewbacca, however. Other than this slight anti-Wookie bias, she is consistently good throughout the original trilogy. She wears white through most of these films, perhaps as a symbol of her goodness, but she is neither naïve nor innocent. She is firmly against the Empire from the beginning, and faces its evil head-on. She sees her home destroyed and she is tortured, yet does not waver in her determination. Remember that this was in the era before Xena, Buffy and the Power Puff Girls. It could be argued that Leia was instrumental in beginning the current era of powerful female heroines.

Leia is also a princess in name only, for her kingdom (the planet Alderan) and most of her subjects, are destroyed earlier on in *A New Hope*, and while she is occasionally addressed as "Princess" after that, she fights for the restoration of a republic, not a monarchy, as one commoner among others. I will even go so far as defend what others have seen as Leia's greatest moment of ignominy- the infamous "brass bikini."

When captured by Jabba the Hutt after her brave attempt to free Han Solo, Leia is dressed in a variant of the chain mail bikini, notorious from the covers of pulp fantasy novels. However, it is because this is a sexist, titillating cliché that what comes after is laudable. In a *New Hope* Lucas turns one stereotype on its head- when Luke opens Leia's cell door to rescue her from the Death Star, for one moment as she lies in repose she could be the heroine of a Sir Walter Scott novel, as painted by Edmund Blair Leighton. Yet immediately thereafter she breaks the romantic spell by insulting Luke- "Aren't you a little short for a Stormtrooper?" and taking charge of her own rescue- hardly the damsel in distress.

Leia's brass bikini in *Return of the Jedi* is setting up the same treatment for the chivalric maiden's darker cousin. For in this outfit she is no longer seen as the chaste object of the courtly love of a Knight of the Round Table, but is dressed as the more blatantly sexual woman from the branch of sword and sorcery that celebrates the anti-hero, of Robert E. Howard's Conan, Fritz Lieber's Fafhrd and the Grey Mouser, and their ilk. Such women, painted for the covers of pulp novels or magazines by Frank Frazetta or one of his countless imitators, are more often harem girls or prostitutes than princesses, and are often surrounded by, or even draped across, the piles of gold and jewels that the protagonists can win upon defeating the warlord that keeps them captive, thus blatantly identifying them as sexual loot to be won.

However, Leia once again overturns a stereotype and the audience's expectations by not waiting for the hero to strike the chains of bondage from her wrists, but instead uses those chains as the means of her liberation. When she strangles Jabba with his own chain, she no longer resembles the slave girl of Frazetta as much as she does Artemisia Gentileschi's *Judith Slaying Holofernes*.

Some would argue that while Leia has her

moments like this, her character is not consistently strong throughout the original trilogy. Indeed, she spends some of the films passively waiting for the male characters to act, though I suspect this neglect was not conscious on Lucas' part, -it appears more as if he put her character on a shelf and forgot about her. Even the romance novel heroine's one crucial choice- which man should she be with- is stripped from her by the expedient of the revelation of her kinship to Luke. Nevertheless, if not perfect, Leia was in the vanguard of a wave of strong female heroes. In comparison to Amidala's own contemporaries, women characters twenty years into that wave,- Xena, Buffy, etc.,- Amidala is unequivocally a step backwards.

Queen Padme Amidala starts in the mold of Leia, but does not follow through in that tradition. Most of her time is spent following the male heroes around. She is a more appealing and more active character when she is masquerading as her own handmaiden, but she abandons this subterfuge midway through the first film. She does engage in some combat, but mostly to save her own skin, not to fight against greater evil. Her greatest weakness however, is her unquestioning allegiance to and love for Anakin.

Amidala falls in love with Anakin in the second of the prequels for no good reason, as he is already obnoxious, surly and self-centered. Puberty has not been kind to Anakin, for in the first film he is a somewhat bland if affable young boy, but in the intervening ten years he has grown into a whiny, self-important little snot. It is unclear why Padme would fall in love with him, yet she does. More significantly, Anakin confesses to her that he has committed atrocities by slaying women and children (presumably non-combatants) of the Sand People in revenge for their killing of his mother. Rather than recoiling in horror from this dangerous psychopath, Amidala marries him. From this point on, her fate is sealed as victim of her love for the wrong man, rather than as any sort of heroic figure.

Amidala expresses disbelief that Anakin could have killed the young Jedi, even though he has already confessed to her to having slain the children of the Tusken Raiders. This level of denial is typical of a seriously abusive relationship, and Amidala is Anakin's enabler.

She dies not in a noble sacrifice in fighting evil, but as a victim of spousal abuse. Now, there is certainly a place in cinema for tragic stories of women who are fatally unable to extricate themselves from abusive relationships, but this is a poor choice of hero for a Star Wars film.

Much of the frustration over the failure of the Star Wars prequels hinges on the squandered opportunities. Granted that if the choice is made to focus the prequels on Anakin, and the birth of Luke and Leia, then obviously the mother of Luke and Leia would need to be included as a character. However, other than the role as mother, Lucas had a blank slate on which to create this character. Amidala could have been so much more than a tragic love interest. Why could she not have been a Jedi, fighting side by side with Anakin, only to have to be slain by him in an epic lightsaber battle, in which she sacrifices herself to protect others? Or she could have been a Sith, a seductive villain, leading him to the Dark Side.

Instead, Amidala is a monarch, who spends a fair amount of time in elaborate dress and makeup. Lucas appears to have had second thoughts about having a monarch as a lead character, for while she is Queen Amidala in the *Phantom Menace,* in *Attack of the Clones,* it is revealed that the throne of Naboo is an elected position, Amidala's term has expired, and a new Queen, Queen Jamillia sits upon the throne.

After losing the throne, Amidala is appointed Senator from Naboo to the Galactic Senate, where she is ineffectual. She spends the remaining two films rather passively, being manipulated by Palapatine and protected by the Jedi. She has one fight scene in the arena, but must ultimately be saved by the Jedi and clone army. This is a far cry from Leia taking over her own rescue in *A New Hope.*

This brings up a larger issue, that is the role of women in the Star Wars films. Let us submit them to what has come to be called the "Bechdel Test." This is named for cartoonist Alison Bechdel, from a strip in her comic, *Dykes to Watch Out For.* In this strip, one of her characters announces that she has three criteria for seeing a film- one, there must be more than one female character, two, the women must talk to each other, and three, that the women must talk to each other about a subject other than men. The punch line of the strip is that the last movie the woman saw that met these criteria is *Aliens,* during which the two women talk to each other about the monster.

A rigorous application of the Bechdel Test to all of the Star Wars films would produce disappointing results. There are on average fewer than two named female characters with speaking parts in the films, and they rarely, if ever interact with each other. Besides Padme and Leia, there are only five other named female speaking roles in the six films- Shmi Skywalker, (Anakin's mother) Sabe, (Padme's handmaiden,) Beru Lars (Luke's aunt), Mon Mothma (leader of the Rebel Alliance) and Queen Jamillia.

Though I would argue that there are plenty of worthwhile films that would fail the Bechdel test, (especially those that deal with real-world situations in which an artificial sex-segregation has been imposed, such as a men's prison, some military units, even the 1950's jury room of *Twelve Angry Men)* and a too-rigorous application becomes merely an exercise in trivia, it is a useful tool for realizing the extent to which film makers, and that would include Lucas, think of the male as the default setting for the human race. Too often in film, all characters are assumed to be male, unless they are to serve as the romantic or sexual interest of the male leads. Sadly, Amidala falls into this category as well. Her functions are to be damsel in distress, forbidden fruit, and mother who dies immediately after childbirth, once her sole important function for the plot is complete.

Lucas' assumption of maleness is evident in that there are several new characters created in the prequels, none of which had to be male. It is even established that women can be Jedi, as we see a few female Jedi as extras. Yet all of the major Jedi - Qui-Gon Jinn, Mace Windu, Obi-Wan, Yoda, - are male, as well as the major antagonists- Darth Maul, Palpatine, General Grievous, Count Dooku, and Jango Fett. (There is one female assassin, Zam Wessel, and some of the Jedi council are female, but none of them have lines.)

It has also been alleged that Lucas only included female Jedi in the films after public critique of their absence, but he still has not placed them in prominent roles. This is quite similar to the addition of Lando Calrissian to *Empire Strikes Back,* in response to the criticism of what had been an all-white Star Wars universe in *A New Hope.*

Further, while the Jedi in the original films seek a zen-like detachment, Lucas adds a further component of monkish celibacy to the Jedi code in the prequels. Perhaps this is intended to make them more like Christian or Buddhist monks, but as Lucas is creating his own world, he could have taken an opportunity to create a sex-positive form of spirituality, but he does not. Presumably this restriction is added to create further conflict by making Anakin and Amidala's love illicit, but as they are never confronted by anyone over this, it adds little to the drama.

This unnecessary anti-sex element combined with the paucity of strong female characters in the prequels is suggestive of a regressive unease with women on Lucas' part, which is all the more unsettling from the same artist who created the great feminist hero, Princess Leia. Yet I will refrain from further psycho-analysis of Lucas, as it is only his films, not his psyche that we have access to.

"Video Gametic"

The term "toyetic" is marketing jargon for the adaptability of an artwork, such as a film, into toys, such as action figures. The original Star Wars films were extremely toyetic, obviously, having sold billions of dollars worth of toys. In its worst manifestations in seeking a highly toyetic property, films will be crafted from their inception to sell toys, at which point art and story telling take second place to toy marketing.

The pod race sequence in *Phantom Menace* suggests a derived neologism "Video gametic." This is the adaptability of film to a video game, possibly intentionally designed with that purpose in mind. The pod race clearly fits this bill- and the story telling suffers for it. It is an unnecessarily long scene, including three circuits of the same course, and does little to advance the plot or establish character. We already know that Anakin is strong in the Force, and there is no doubt that he will win, and thus enable the party to leave the planet. While there is little tension in this scene, it does shout its advertisement for a pod-race video game. Predictably the pod-race video game *Star Wars Episode 1: Racer* was released in 1999.

There are many other "video gametic" scenes throughout the prequels, such as Padme's travels through the droid factory on Genosan. One can almost see the game player hunched over his or her game controller, timing Padme's steps just right to avoid the obstacles.

Too Much CGI

The heavy presence of computer generated imagery, rather than the elaborate physical sets, models, and costumes of the original trilogy, also adds to the feeling that one is not so much watching a film as watching someone else play a video game. This also contributes to the films frenetic pace and cluttered look. When new ships can be added to a battle with a click of the mouse, why not add dozens more?

In the *Return of the Jedi,* there is a sequence in the climactic battle scene when the rebel pilots realize that they have entered a trap, and wave upon wave of tie-fighters swoop down upon us, and the pilots. This is many more ships than the squads of only a dozen or so that we have seen up to this point in all of the first three movies. As such, it conveys an emotional impression- we are both impressed with the effort to create the effects, and are vicariously afraid for our heroes, as they realize they are outnumbered and in grave danger.

Unfortunately for the prequels, every battle is as stuffed to the gills as this one, resulting not in greater excitement, but a numbing effect. For much of these films, the same is true- three tie fighters bearing down on Luke's lone x-wing in *A New Hope* had us on the edge of our seats, in part because we were emotionally involved with these characters. Hordes of nameless ships, battle droids and clones blowing each other up ad nauseum does not engage the audience's emotional interest. Lucas makes the mistake, common to many current film makers, of mistaking motion for action. Charlie Bucket taking an Everlasting Gobstopper out of his pocket and placing it on the table is action. The pod race is merely motion.

Sanitized Violence

The CGI also contributes to the sanitizing of violence in the prequels. In the original films, characters with distinct personalities whom we care about are killed- Luke's parents, his childhood friend Biggs. Even "redshirts", minor characters who die quickly are given names- "We lost Tyree, lost Hutch,"- which evokes a whole, though unstated, history. Even in the victorious battle of the Ewoks over the Stormtroopers in *Return of the Jedi,* the camera lingers over one dead Ewok, as his friend tries, pathetically, to coax him to get up.

In the prequels, however, most casualties are faceless, nameless and interchangeable droids, clones and Gungans, the latter's computer generated homogeneity rendering them as emotionally sympathetic as the alien ships blown up in a game of *Space Invaders.* Indeed, Lucas' reliance on computer generated scenery rather than sets and location shoots robs the prequels of the sense of exotic place that Hoth or Dagobah had in the original trilogy. Naboo's too perfect green lawns and blue skies make us feel not that we are on a foreign planet, but merely trapped in a video game.

One of the oldest philosophical arguments within science fiction regards the sentience of artificial intelligences, such as robots and computers. Can a robot think? Can a robot feel? Or, as in the title of Phillip K. Dick's novel, do androids dream of electric sheep? Perhaps the earliest expression of this question is offered by L.Frank Baum when his robot, Tik-Tok the clockwork man, is asked if he can feel.

Tik-Tok has springs for walking, speaking and thinking, but when he is asked if he can feel, he replies that though he may act as if he does, he only does so because "he is wound up that way" i.e. he is programmed to act as if he has emotions, even though he really doesn't. This discussion, in Baum's *Ozma of Oz,* (1907) predates even the invention of the word "Robot" by Karel Čapek in 1921 in his play *R.U.R. (Rossum's Universal Robots)*

Many other science fiction writers since Baum - Čapek, Asimov, Dick, etc,- have answered the question in the affirmative, that computers and robots of sufficient complexity will achieve true intelligence and sentience, which raises questions of their proper ethical treatment, their rights, etc. The mathematician Alan Turing proposed the now-famous Turing Test of artificial intelligence- that it will be achieved when computers can have a conversation with a person that is indistinguishable from that of another human being. Arguably, this test has now been passed. I would like to suggest an alternative benchmark for artificial sentience, not intelligence, i.e. self awareness or emotion. That will be achieved when computers can express free will- as evidenced when a computer or robot says- "I don't want to do that."

In the original Star Wars trilogy, droids have achieved this level of sentience- they not only think, but they feel, they have emotions and personalities. C-3PO and R2D2 express emotions such as pride, fear and annoyance. For but one example, both express empathy towards Leia as they await Luke, feared lost on Hoth. Other droids in the original trilogy are rude, cowardly, or even feel pain when tortured.

Yet in the prequels, Obi-Wan dismisses all of this when he denies that droids can think. This may be appropriate for the elitism that underlies the prequels, but it would seem to contradict the originals. It is convenient however, for Lucas' sanitizing of the violence of the prequels, for if droids can't really think or feel, then it doesn't matter when they are destroyed, and they can serve as expendable cannon fodder.

Paving Coruscant

In the course of his investigation of the assassination attempt in *Attack of the Clones,* Obi-wan takes on the role of a detective, and the plot becomes that of a 20th century police procedural. This bit is laced with jarring anachronisms. While bars and restaurants may be assumed to be fairly universal, 1950's style American diners are not, and despite a thin veneer of sci-fi exoticism- a robot waitress and a many armed alien chef, - it remains jarringly out of place in a "galaxy far, far away." Similarly inappropriate, Obi-wan encounters a drug dealer- also an artifact of the late 20th century, and not in keeping with the established world view as the existence of recreational pharmaceuticals, and their illegality, has never been hinted at in the four films prior to this. For a brief interlude, it adds little, yet suggests a lack of imagination on the part of the writers, an inability to look beyond their immediate world.

Yet another example is that the Pod Race is accompanied by an announcer- providing commentary as would a twentieth century sportscaster. This is doubly off-putting as it is not only stylistically anachronistic, but it is perhaps the only example we see in all of the six films of anything approaching mass communication. It is perhaps illogical that though we see holographic messages between individuals, there are no newscasts or other large scale publishing- even though it would be useful for the various political factions. However, once this is established as the norm, (and it is in keeping with the tone of the films as fantasy dressed as science fiction) it makes less sense to violate it this one time. Despite the superficial attempt at making the announcer exotic- he has two heads- he is still an uncreatively Twentieth-century American anachronism.

Science Fiction author Ursula K. LeQuin addressed this phenomenon in her classic essay "From Elf Land to Poughkeepsie". She distinguishes between truly creative fantasy and science fiction, that creates rich, complex new worlds, and more hackneyed works that only put a superficial exotic gloss on otherwise mundane, modern stories. The former require more work on the part of the reader, but are ultimately more rewarding, while the latter are more accessible to a general audience, but do not use the full opportunities for innovation that these genres present. She uses the analogy of "paving Yellowstone" that is, visiting Yellowstone National Park before and after roads were added. The experience of backpacking into Yellowstone is not the same as driving through by car, especially when bringing along all the comforts of home. She argues that a good science fiction or fantasy writer should make the reader feel the difference and strangeness of their new world- otherwise there is no point in writing in this genre, just as there is no point in going to Yellowstone if you never leave your R.V. Why bother taking us to the alien world of Coruscant if it is just like Twentieth-century America?

(This phenomenon is closely linked to the idea of "authenticity" as articulated by Walter Benjamin in his seminal essay "Art in the Age of Mechanical Reproduction," though space precludes a thorough discussion of that connection here.)

Lucas has failed to make us feel that strangeness in *Attack of the Clones.* Compare its diner to the cantina sequence in *A New Hope.* The cantina was full of menace, and exotic creatures who looked strange and acted unpredictably. Because of their strangeness, Lucas is also able to include a pithy bit of social commentary, when the barkeep refuses to serve droids. In the diner, the characters may have the external trappings of aliens and robots, but act exactly as twentieth century Americans, with the droid waitress even having a Brooklyn accent.

The original trilogy created a new vocabulary to give names to new creatures and races- Wookies, Ewoks, taun-tauns, etc. In the prequels, however, Lucas adds unnecessary new words for old concepts in a stilted attempt at creating an exotic feel that is otherwise lacking. Thus an apprentice is a "padwan learner", though the word "apprentice" would suffice as it does in the original trilogy. Children are now "younglings" even though there is nothing distinguishing these children from any others. This last change might be an attempt at softening the atrocities of Anakin, for the "younglings" we encounter are slain by Anakin.

Inconsistencies Between the Two Sets of Films.

Many fans have pointed out continuity problems between the two sets of films. The source of many of these flaws is the lack of creativity on Lucas' part in locating much of the action of the prequels on the planet of Tatooine, involving the extended Skywalker family. Lucas leaves C-3PO on Tatooine for ten years between *Phantom Menace* and *Attack of the Clones.* During this time he lives with Luke's mother and her step-son, Owen Lars. Lucas is aware enough of the potential inconsistencies of this that at the end of *Revenge of the Sith,* Senator Organa orders C-3PO's memory to be wiped, so that the C-3PO's ignorance of Tatooine in *A New Hope* will make sense.

However, Owen's memory has not been wiped, yet he does not recognize C-3PO when Owen, (now Luke's Uncle Owen) purchases him from the Jawas in *A New Hope.* Just as nonsensically, while Obi-wan adventures with R2-D2 throughout the prequels, in *A New Hope,* he not only does not recognize R2, but claims that he has never owned a droid.

Lucas ends the *Revenge of the Sith* with an image of the Death Star beginning construction, as if to wink at the audience- "Remember this, and how cool and scary it is? You'll see this again in the originals" It takes nearly twenty years for the station to be built, the time it takes Luke to grow to maturity between the two sets of trilogies. Yet the Second Death Star is built in only the time between *A New Hope* and *Return of the Jedi,* a year or two at most.

Ben suggests in *Empire* that he was not much younger than Luke when he began training, but the prequels have the Jedi start training as very young children.

Ben hides Luke from his father, Anakin by hiding him with Anakin's own step brother on his home planet. Vader must not have been looking very hard to find them. This is yet another example of Lucas recycling key elements from the first trilogy, rather than creating new planets, characters, villains, etc.

There are numerous other such inconsistencies, but the examples above should suffice to demonstrate the lack of continuity or consistency. While these may seem to the casual viewer as merely an exercise in trivial nitpicking, it indicates that Lucas has not put the serious thought into the films that any artist owes his creation, and his audience.

Signs of Worse to Come.

Many devoted fans saw, or should have seen, the signs that Lucas had lost sight of the important elements of his creation when he released the "special editions" of the original trilogy, in 1997. Lucas, apparently dazzled by the advances in CGI technology, (some of which he developed, through his special effects company, Industrial Light and Magic) cluttered the original films with extra and unnecessary spaceships, aliens, and droids, seemingly just because he could. Moreover, he had opportunity to add scenes that had been edited out, and in one case, grievously alter one pre-existing scene. Yet the choices he made in doing so were awkward, presaging the crap that was to come in the prequels.

For example, he added back in a scene to *A New Hope* in which Jabba confronts Han Solo on Tatooine. Filmed before the appearance of Jabba in *Return of the Jedi,* this was originally shot with a human actor. For the special edition, a computer generated image of Jabba is laid over the image of the actor. This scene doesn't work for a number of reasons. One, the original human actor was much smaller than the creature created for *Return of the Jedi,* so the CGI version is significantly smaller than the Jabba we see later in *Jedi.* More importantly, the interaction between the two characters is not in keeping with the character of Jabba that has been established in

Jedi. Rather than the intimidating figure that can resist Luke's Jedi mind powers and has people killed for his amusement, the *New Hope* Jabba is bullied and blustered by Han. Han even steps on Jabba's tail in front of his lackies without receiving any punishment from Jabba. Once again, Lucas seems unaware that by diminishing the villains of a piece, you also diminish the heroes, a flaw found throughout the prequels.

Lucas did restore one scene that improved a *New Hope,* but inexplicably did not include its companion piece. Luke meets up with his friend from Tattoine, Biggs, among the rebel fighter pilots on the Moon of Yavin prior to the battle of the Death Star. Biggs then dies in that battle. In the original theatrical release, the scene of the two reuniting prior to the battle was cut, so that when Biggs dies in the midst of the battle, the importance of this to Luke is unclear. (Sadly, Mark Hamill does little to sell this emotion in the scene, either.)

However, their reuniting scene is brief, and would have benefited from the re-inclusion of the earlier scene on Tattoine, shot but edited out of the original release, where Biggs tells Luke that he is about to jump ship and join the Rebellion. Biggs encourages Luke to join the rebellion as well, but Luke defers, citing his uncle Owen's need for him on the farm. Thus, when later in the film Luke's aunt and uncle are killed, Luke is willing to join Obi-Wan and leave Tatooine- "There's nothing here for me now." It is unclear why Lucas neglected to include this scene, with its potential for both setting up Luke's growth as a character, and, more importantly, making Biggs' death in the assault on the Death Star more consequential

The most egregious, and talked about, change in the special edition is in a confrontation in the Mos Eisley Cantina between Han Solo and a bounty hunter named Greedo. In the original version, Greedo accosts Han at gunpoint. After Greedo threatens to kill him, Han sneakily shoots Greedo under the table, and then casually flips a coin to the bartender, apologizing with a quick "sorry about the mess."

In the special edition, Lucas has added in a shot coming from Greedo's gun before Han shoots. This both minimizes the menace of Greedo, as he is somehow unable to hit a man-sized target from a few feet away, and waters down Han's character as a "scoundrel". Apparently, Lucas has failed to grasp the importance of Han's character development. (I will return to the importance of this development later.) A close reading of the changes made in the re-releases of the classic trilogy will show that Lucas has begun to stray away form the trope that underlay the works.

(This self-bowdlerization by Lucas is an unfortunate consequence of the abilities of CGI and the re-release of films both to theaters and on DVD. Perhaps just as heinous of an example is Spielberg's computer "airbrushing" out the firearms of federal agents in *E.T.*, and replacing them with walkie-talkies. He no longer felt comfortable having the menacing government agents pointing guns at minors in E.T., even though feds pointing guns at kids is a daily occurrence in the real world, and they are the villains of the film. This is suggetive of Spielberg's reactionary response to the events of September 11th, 2001. Prior to that date, Spielberg had said he would never portray aliens in a negative light, but after that date, he produced a remake of *War of the Worlds*. If the events of September 11th changed one's world view, then one was terribly ignorant of the world prior to that date. It appears that Spielberg may have grown more conservative as he ages, as the anti-intellectual, militaristic *Saving Private Ryan* would attest.)

The Dual Dualities of the Force

There are significant changes between the Force as it is described in the first three films, and as it is in the prequels. One of these changes is the unnecessary introduction of the midichlorians as the source of the Force. These mitochondria-like particles are abruptly offered up as the cause of the Force. Strangely, no mention of these were made by Kenobi or Yoda while explaining the Force to Luke in the first three films. They are clearly introduced as a plot device merely to provide an "objective" measure of the Force. Qui Gon Jin is so impressed with Anakin's midichlorian count to remove him from his mother for Jedi training, and to continue training him over the objections of Yoda and the Jedi Council.

This cheapens and trivializes the nature of the Force, from something of a spiritual and universal character, which "connects all living things" and both "guides" and "obeys" the Jedi, to something merely akin to psychic power or mana. This also buttresses one of the more troubling elements of the Force, which is only hinted at in the original films- its aristocratic nature. While it has been established that the Force runs in families, it is also suggested that it permeates all things, and that it is not necessarily off limits to anyone- indeed, Ben Kenobi attempts to instruct Han Solo in the basics of the Force, only to be rebuffed. Instead, in the prequels, the Force is far more elitist, and the Jedi are much more guarded about who they teach- which makes sense if one can only be born to the Force.

Further, by making the Force an observable, measurable power with the midichlorians, it removes the element of philosophical belief from the Force. In the original trilogy, Luke is exhorted to "trust the Force" by Kenobi. He fails to levitate his ship, and when Yoda succeeds, Luke says "I don't believe it," to which Yoda replies "and that is why you failed." Yet, in the prequels, the Force is no longer a matter of belief, (and the moral and philosophical growth that Luke must go through to have that belief) but can simply be measured with a blood test.

There is another difference, even greater than the midichlorians, between the conception of the Force in the two trilogies. Both series talk of a duality to the Force- it has both a light and dark side. Superficially, this resemble the yin/yang concept of Taoism. Despite rhetoric of Yoda or Ben Kenobi that describes the Force flowing through one like chi, or of one following the Force like the "way" of Taoism, the resemblance is only superficial in the original trilogy. The Force of the original films is more Zoroastrian or Manichean than it is Taoist.

Western culture has its tradition of duality, but it differs greatly from the Eastern concept of Taosim. Western religious beliefs often contain the idea that life is a struggle between two opposing Forces of good and evil. One of the earliest manifestations of this is in Zorastrianism, which developed in Persia from the early first millenium BC. In Zorastrianism the all-good creator god, Ahura Mazda battles the evil Force of chaos, Angra Mainyu. The two are not equal, however, and Ahura Mazda will defeat Angra Mainyu at the end of time.

This entered into the Abrahamic tradition around the time of Christ, and Christianity continues this tradition of existence as a battle of good versus evil. God, the angels and saints, are fighting against Satan and his devils for the souls of humanity. Manicheanism, one of the Gnostic faiths of the 3rd century AD further elaborated this conflict as between a spirit realm and the material world. Possibly its most extreme form was that of the Neo- Manicheans, Christian movements during the middle ages that saw all of existence as either good or evil, and the realm of spirit as good, and the world of the flesh as evil.

Chinese philosophy, in contrast, sees Yin and Yang as two equal Forces of nature, morally neutral. A prosperous and healthy life can be achieved through a successful balance of the two Forces.

To starkly contrast these western and eastern

dualities, a Christian priest would never diagnosis a parishioner's spiritual problems as resulting from an excess of Christ and a deficit of Satan, and would never proscribe more Satan to balance out God. A Taoist might very well say that some one suffers from an excess of yang energy and needs to counter it with more yin.

The dual nature of the Force in the original three films, is firmly in the Western, Zorastrian style of duality. The dark side is portrayed as evil- seductive, easy and destructive. It is the realm of anger and selfishness, and is to be avoided at all costs. While the Dark Side is more seductive, it is ultimately not more powerful than the light side. Yoda would never counsel Luke that he is deficient in the Dark Side, and so he should seek out some more Darkness to balance his light.

However, in the prequels, rather than seeking to avoid the dark side, there is now an emphasis on balancing the two sides of the Force. The Jedi Council speaks of a prophecy of a "chosen one" who is not to vanquish the dark side, but who is simply to "bring balance" to the Force. It is unclear where this prophecy comes from, which introduces yet another inconsistency between the two trilogies, as there are no prophecies within the original. It is also unclear as to what was imbalanced about the status quo. Were the Jedi too *good* before the arrival of the chosen one?

This concept of the Force superficially resembles Taoism, whose "dark side" is not evil, but merely male to female, active to passive, hot to cold, etc. Yet, this Dark Side is not the yang of Taoism, however the prequels might attempt to portray it as such. The Dark Side is evil- it is shown through both sets of films to lead one to murder, torture, betrayal, slaughtering of children and genocide. It is morally and intellectually vacuous to suggest such a Force need merely to be "balanced." Should a moderate amount of torture and genocide be encouraged, as long as it is balanced by an equal amount of good? A close reading reveals that the Jedi of the two trilogies would give different answers to this question.

Some may argue that a balance between good and evil is desirable. This fails on two counts- one if that balance is itself desirable, it would therefore be good- in which case the balanced state between good and evil would itself be good, thus tipping the scales toward good, in which case it would then need to be balanced by a certain amount of imbalance- though perhaps this state's own imbalancing would suffice to re-balance things- which would then be good, again throwing things out of balance. Such a paradoxical progression can continue infinitely.

More seriously though, some argue that evil is necessary for good to exist. If we did not have temptation, then resisting that temptation would not be laudable. For the exercise of free will for the good to be possible, the ability to exercise it for evil must also exist. (This argument, of course, has existed in philosophy for millennia. When God's allowance of the exercise of free will is added to the mix, it is referred to as the problem of evil or theodicy.)

Given that the potential for good action necessitates the *potential* for evil, nowhere does this necessitate an *equal* amount of evil. Let us take, for example, murder- an evil act. Granted that many, if not all people are tempted by anger, greed, lust, etc to commit murder, - or at least assault someone in a way that might result in their death, the resisting of this temptation is a good action, the more serious the temptation, the greater the good of its resistance. For these good actions to exist, the real possibility of murder must exist, one could even posit that at least one murder must be committed to maintain the possibility that murders can actually be committed. However, it is insane to posit that it is desirable for the number of times that people resist these temptations only be equal to the number of murders that are committed- that is, for every one hundred people seriously tempted to commit murder, that fifty resist and fifty commit the crime. Only a psychopath would argue that a ratio of forty murders to sixty people who restrain themselves is too low, and that to "restore balance" ten more people should have chosen to kill. Yet this is what follows from "balancing" the Dark Side of the Force, which is shown to lead to murder, torture and mass destruction. Even if the potential of the Dark Side is necessary to define the Light, for that potential to be realized in an equal amount to that by which it is resisted is desirable only to the truly evil.

(I am curious how this radical revamping of the Force and the Jedi religion would affect its modern day followers. There are people around the world who claim to follow the "Church of the Jedi." While some of these may be in jest, -and there is some evidence that those who claimed "Jedi" on a British religious survey were doing so in protest of the intrusiveness of the survey- it also appears that many are sincere in their belief. Assuming that some of its adherents are sincere, the radical changes in the faith between the two trilogies should have resulted in schisms. I have attempted to contact modern day followers of the Jedi Faith, to get their reaction to the "new testament" of their faith that is the prequels. The only response I received indicated that the films are but an inspiration, not dogma, and so could be easily reconciled. Indeed, it appears that the films are merely a jumping off point for a synchretic process of integrating Buddhist, Taoist and other philosophies into the modern day Jedi faith. The one response I did receive reconciled the two trilogies by suggesting that they both addressed people's responses to suffering. However that is so broad as to include nearly any work of literature or art ever created.)

The Jedi

The change in the character of the Force is accompanied by a change in the nature of the Jedi. In *A New Hope* Obi-wan describes the Jedi as having brought "peace and justice" to the galaxy for a thousand years. The Jedi of the prequels bear little resemblance to this ideal.

For example, in *The Phantom Menace,* Qui-Gon Jinn tells Anakin that he has not come to Tatooine to free slaves. Well, why the hell not? What greater injustice than slavery is there? It could be seen as a personal failing on Jinn's part, as he is more obsessed by the potential power of Anakin's Midichlorians that with fighting injustice, but the Jedi as a whole are not crusading to end slavery, either. In fact, in the subsequent films, the Jedi appear to endorse slavery and own slaves themselves- the Clone Army.

The decision of the Jedi to use the clone army is accompanied with very little debate. Not only are the supposedly wise Jedi completely duped (it will be revealed that this is part of an elaborate trap) but they are seemingly unconcerned with the ethics of owning and using an army of apparent slaves.

The screenwriters seem to be suffering from a similar delusion, or lack of comprehension about the nature of clones. Merely because an individual is created artificially does not mean that that individual is somehow less than human, or has less than a free will. (Recognizing these prejudices in art is not merely academic, as cloned humans may already exist, and certainly will do so within the life times of those raised on these films.) These clones are also genetically engineered to be automatons, obeying orders like robots, and treated as mere possessions- they are not asked if they wish to fight, but are instead treated like chattel. Indeed, they are paid for by the Jedi, and accepted as a shipment of presumably, enslaved warriors.

Further, in the Clone Wars, the Jedi serve the Republic against the Separatists with unflagging loyalty- for no good reason. Why the Jedi should feel particularly loyal to the Republic versus the Separatists, and why they should be willing to fight on the side of one over the other is never adequately explained. It is a political truism that one man's "terrorist" is another's "freedom fighter." The "Separatists" are the "Rebels" of the prequels, and they might be presumed to have legitimate reasons for wanting to secede from the Republic. Count Dooku, himself a Jedi, seems to think so. Since many planets freely join the Separatists, it would suggest that they have legitimate grievances, yet rather than try to negotiate either peaceful secession or reconciliation, the Jedi only use military force to stymie their right to self determination. The Jedi don't even have Lincoln's *post-hoc* justification of liberating slaves for ruthlessly suppressing secessionists.

Similarly, the Old Republic is held up in the original films as something worthwhile and laudable- we are dismayed when it is announced that the Emperor has finally dissolved the Senate in *A New Hope.* The rebel's goal is to restore the Republic, and as they are presented as heroic for doing so, it is reasonable to expect that the Republic is something worth restoring. In yet another example of squandered potential, rather than presenting us with a Republic in the prequels that is worth morning the loss of, the Republic is ineffectual, indifferent and incompetent. It seems that Lucas, in the case of both the Jedi and the Old Republic, is incapable of creating characters that lose, who are not also losers.

Another trend in the Jedis throughout the prequels- most of their actions serve only to benefit themselves, and have little, if any benefit to the rest of the galaxy. Indeed, because of their discovery and training of Anakin, they seem to have brought mostly evil into the world.

They are also not very wise. The Jedi council have their misgivings about both Anakin and the Emperor, but are too indecisive to do anything about either until it is too late, and are impotent to prevent their evil. The transparent ruse that Darth Sideous and Senator Palpatine are not the same person does not fool any audience member. In what was clearly supposed to be dramatic, when the Palpatine reveals himself to be the Sith Lord, it only elicits yawns from the audience, yet the supposedly wise Jedi haven't a clue.

It may have been Lucas' intention to tell a tragedy of the Jedi having fallen from their grandeur for having turned their backs on their ideals, but if this was his intent, it fails in the telling. If that were the story he wished to tell, he could have had a hero struggle against this decay and corruption. Instead it is only the villains of the piece which are aware of it, and the supposed "heroes" are indifferent to, or unaware of, their own decay.

Another change in the nature of the Jedi is the aforementioned celibacy. To add to the drama of Anakin and Amidala's romance, a heretofore unknown aspect of Jedi dogma is added- that the "Jedi Code" - also not mentioned in the previous four films- mandates celibacy of the Jedi. There is no effort made to explain why this prohibition would flow from the nature of the Force, or Jedi beliefs. While Jedi belief prior to this had a strong sense of good and evil, it did not share the Christian idea, most strongly held in Manicheanism, that the flesh, and sex were evil or corrupting. Indeed, while the Jedi had previously emphasized the power of the will over the body, they also stressed physical mastery, not a rejection of the body.

Moreover, in the first films, there is no indication that Luke's interest in Leia is anyway in conflict with his Jedi training. In *Empire Strikes Back*, Luke is warned not to attempt to rescue Leia, but this is because his training is incomplete, and it is likely a trap. There is no sense that love or sex themselves are evil or dangerous. Yet in *Attack of the Clones*, Anakin's love is now taboo, both presumably to add to the romance, and, probably less intentionally, to make him more of a selfish, deceitful twit.

In a related plot hole, it is not explained why, if Anakin loved his mother so much, he did nothing in the past ten years between *Phantom Menace* and *Attack of the Clones* to free her from a life of poverty and slavery on Tatooine. Did the Jedi forbid him for some unknown reason? What part of the Jedi code forbids the Jedi from freeing slaves? Though now an adult, did he not have enough freedom of movement to save his mother? Or, as I suspect, did the writers just not think it through?

The Jedi as presented in the original trilogy are noble and good, those of the prequels are foolish and incompetent. This inconsistency can be accounted for in three ways. The first explanation, and the simplest, is that Lucas merely did not put sufficient thought into the work and was not aware of the contradictions he was creating. This is my contention, and I think it primarily results from an inability on Lucas' part to write tragic heroes- characters who are good and noble, and yet fail. For the Jedi of the prequels are not heroes with a tragic flaw, but are flawed, limited characters lacking any heroism.

Apologists for Lucas, however will argue that these contradictions are intentional. Perhaps Lucas had a change of heart between making the first trilogy and the prequels. Perhaps he came to accept a radical post-modern critique of morality and truth and set out to undermine the Jedi as the heroes he had created them to be in the first films. If so, he handles this retroactive condemning of his heroes with the same adroitness as his clumsy attempt to have Greedo shoot first- it lessons his heroes, while adding nothing of value to the story.

Some will argue even further that this was Lucas' intention from the beginning, and that he set up the Jedi as heroes in the original trilogy only so that he could later reveal them to have not just feet of clay, but entire bodies made thereof. Proponents of this theory point to the equivocations made by Obi-wan, in *Return of the Jedi* when explaining why he did not reveal Luke's parentage to him. They would argue that this flaw on Kenobi's point was intended to subtly introduce the idea that the Jedi were not as good as they claimed, later brought to fruition in the prequels.

However, this argument is predicated on the presumption of Lucas' near papal infallibility. I find it much more likely to believe that Obi-wan did not tell Luke that Vader was his father in *A New Hope* because Lucas hadn't yet decided that was the case. It may be near heretical to some, but I think many of these flaws can be most reasonably attributed to Lucas merely making things up as he goes along. The contention that he had all the films carefully mapped out in advanced is belied by, for just one example, the fact that Luke and Leia kiss passionately more than once- it's frankly creepy to think that Lucas planned these knowing ahead of time that they would later be revealed to be brother and sister.

The last explanation- that Lucas intended to condemn the Sith and the Jedi equally across the totality of the films, and that Luke's heroism in *Return of the Jedi* is found by his rejection of both the Sith and the Jedi can only be seriously held by one who is deaf to the tone of the films. The Jedi are presented as heroes throughout the films, Luke explicitly rejects the Dark Side and the Emperor by affirming that "I am a Jedi, like my father," and the end of *Return of the Jedi,* with the smiling spirits of Yoda, Ben and Anakin, is clearly a triumph for the Jedi.

Yet, whatever the motivation,- sloppy thought and writing, a radical mid-life change in philosophy, or a prank that took twenty five years to execute- the effect of this change in the Jedi between the two films is for Lucas to effectively piss all over the characters and philosophy he spent the first three films to build up. It is this effect that may account for the great sense of betrayal felt by many of the original films deepest fans, equatable to being abused by a trusted relative.

Yoda

Yoda made his first appearance in *Empire Strikes Back*, and continued in *Return of the Jedi*. In both of those films, Yoda is a wise Jedi master, humble and self-effacing. Obi-wan's ghost sends Luke to study with Yoda on Dagobah. Yoda instructs Luke in humility, confidence, and mastery of his emotions, in addition to mastery of the Force. When Luke first meets Yoda, unaware of the Jedi master's identity, Luke tells Yoda that he is looking for "a great warrior," to which Yoda replies "Wars not make one great."

Yet in the prequels, Yoda is primarily portrayed as just that, a warrior, and not a great one, either. Because Lucas made the mistake of making the plot of these films the devolution of Anakin into Vader, we only see a Yoda who is powerless to stop these developments. Thus, he has bad feelings about Anakin-sensing "much fear" in him when he is first presented to the Jedi Council, but not doing anything about it. It is as if Yoda is the old fortune teller, warning the protagonists not to investigate the haunted castle on the hill. This might provide foreshadowing, but foreshadowing is an exercise in redundancy in the prequels, as most everyone knows that Anakin will become Vader.

The only other role Yoda has in the prequels is

as a warrior- his computer generated body bounces around the screen, light saber flashing. His little green face contorts in the scowl of a warrior, yet he accomplishes little of greatness, either as a warrior, as a philosopher or as a teacher.

Anakin Christ

One of the odder elements which is added in the prequels and then never adequately followed up on, is that Anakin is the result of a virgin birth. His mother reveals this to Qui-Gon Jinn, and it is suggested that the Midichlorians, like the holy sprirt, came upon her and impregnated her. Given that there is a dark side to the Force, and that the Force is merely Midichlorians, is it possible that there are dark Midichlorians? Why else would the Force seek to create an evil person like Anakin? To fulfill the prophecy of the chosen one who will restore balance to the Force?

Yoda suggests that the prophecy may have been misread- implying that Luke, not Anakin, is the promised one who will restore “balance” to the Force. However, if that imbalance was only caused by his evil father, who was himself created by the Force, it seems like the universe (certainly the billions of residents of Alderan) would have been better off had neither been born at all.

This virgin birth of Anakin is mentioned, but never resolved. Palpatine suggests that his old master knew how to create life, suggesting that either he or his master may have created Anakin, but to what end? The virgin birth as impregnated by Satan? If Anakin was created by the Sith, why then leave him stranded on Tattoine, as a slave child? Did they forget they had created the most powerful life in the galaxy? Was it with the absurd hope that some Jedi years in the future would accidentally crash land on this planet and then rescue the boy, train him as a Jedi, and thus put the boy in the position to later betray the Jedi? Why not either raise the child as a Sith, or, if infiltrating the Jedi was intended, why not present him directly to the Jedi?

It is unclear what Lucas intends to signify by Anakin's virgin birth. Is it, like the Midichlorians, merely a plot device to trick Qui-Gon Jinn and Kenobi into training Anakin? Is it intended as some sort of critique or comment on Christianity? Is Anakin supposed to be some sort of Anti-Christ? Such a powerful allusion should not be casually introduced without making one's point clear. Alas, I suspect it is merely another example of a poorly thought out element thrown into the mix, without a clear idea of where it was leading.

The Past as (Only) Prologue

One main reason for the tedious and convoluted plot of the prequels is that their plots serve only to further a separate end, and are not ends in and of themselves. The three prequels serve to establish four main developments that have occurred by the beginning of Episode 4. These are the change of Senator Palpatine into the Emperor, the concomitant fall of the old Republic and the creation of the Empire,

Anakin's transformation into Darth Vader, and the birth of Luke and Leia. However, the original three films were successful with those events only existing as backstory and brief exposition. It was not necessary to the story that was told in those films to create a three-film prologue. The prequels are unnecessary as prologue, but because they are hobbled to that goal, they fail as independent stories as well.

This last point is particularly telling of a lack of imagination on the part of Lucas and the filmmakers. Lucas backed himself into a corner of his own making. In interviews after the success of the original films, he had established that he had conceived of the Star Wars films as being a lengthy cycle, with three prequels, and three sequels to come after. There had also been hints, greedily jumped on by fans at conventions, in fan 'zines, and eventually over the Internet, as to what the prequels might include- e.g, the Clone Wars, which are mentioned in the original films, hints that Boba Fett's armor was a uniform from those wars, that Darth Vader's armor and breathing apparatus were the result of a fall into a volcano, and that the two Droids were the only characters that would be in all nine films.

Yet Lucas chose to severely limit himself in the prequels. He could have placed any number of stories against the backdrop of these events. He chose to make the protagonists the pre-established characters, with thus no room for growth. Obi-wan, Yoda, Anakin could have all been supporting characters, against which a new and exciting story could have been told.

But he seemingly could not think beyond his already created work. He does introduce supporting characters- Qui Gon and Mace Windu, but since their destinies are shackled to Anakin, all they are able to do is get killed by the bad guys, while accomplishing nothing.

The greatest flaw in this area was to make Anakin the protagonist. Since the audience knows that he would eventually become Darth Vader, there is no surprise in his fall. Yet, it was also handled without any suspense, either. (There are a number of films in which, even though the outcome is already known by the audience, skillful film making can keep the audience emotionally involved. *Milk* and *Heavenly Creatures* are but two examples that come to mind.) By the second prequel, *Attack of the Clones*, Anakin has no redeeming qualities whatsoever. He is petulant, whiny, arrogant, stubborn and yet easily manipulated by Palpatine. His descent into evil is neither shocking or surprising. The only surprising thing is that the Jedi didn't see it coming.

Placing Anakin as the protagonist was a mistake, but had that been a necessity, it could have been done in a such a way as to maintain interest and suspense, and to have an emotional impact on the audience. If one must detail the descent into evil, it is best done as a surprising, heartbreaking tragedy- for example if Anakin had been a heroic, good person, who was only driven to the dark side through some catastrophic tragedy, this could have kept the audience engaged, and crushed when he falls. As it was, even though Padme's death is the final straw, Anakin has been walking in the Dark Side for much longer than the good.

He is not a good man who gives in to temptation and commits a touch of evil, but a deeply selfish man who creates profound evil, ultimately merely to save his wife. Palapatine convinces Anakin that his wife will die, and the only way to save her is to join the Dark Side. In order to save her, he willingly slays Jedi, including children, and assists in the creation of the Empire, ultimately killing millions. Was the sex that good?

Predestination

One of the great problems with these films are that they are prequels in the worst sense of the word. Lucus has created a six-hour prologue to his original works. This means there, is of course, no suspense, as we already know the outcome- who will die, and who must live, and what will become of them. Thus, it would take a great effort to make the telling of the story interesting, which may be why Lucas must distract us with so much flash and bang. More Wookies! More Lightsabers! More Yoda!

Further, because he seeks to tell this story, which must work itself into a predetermined ending, many contrivances must be applied to shoe horn every character to its prearranged ending. Thus the audience as well as the characters are stripped of free will. Thus, Obi-Wan is directed to Tatooine in the first film, because they must meet Anakin there. The Jedi make ridiculous decisions, such as teaching Anakin and giving him privileges, etc, after he repeatedly acts like a complete tool. Further, none of them see through the transparent political maneuvers of Palpatine, though he might as well be twirling a mustache as he does them. Even Obi-wan and Yoda must retreat from the battle against evil, even though they have not been clearly defeated, so that they can patiently assume their places to await the next film. "Go into exile, must I," declares Yoda after fighting Palpatine to a draw. Why he must is left unstated- though the only answer is "because that's where I am in the next movies."

Indeed, this is reflected by the strange addition to the Jedi belief system of "prophecies" and a "chosen one," absent from the original trilogy. As the films themselves cannot escape being prologue, so are their characters trapped by "destiny." Doing so removes the free will from all of the characters, and weakens them considerably. Obi-wan and Yoda give up the fight for no explicable reason, except to wait for a chosen one, a "messiah" even though putting their faith in such a messiah was disastrous the last time they tried it, and while they wait, their evil creation will continue to rampage through the galaxy.

This inability to escape her destiny and lack of free will is the final blow against making Amidala any sort of admirable character. She has one of the best lines in the film, when watching the Senate vote Imperial powers to Palpatine. "So this is how liberty dies. With thunderous applause." A truly heroic character might have added something along the lines of "not if I have anything to say about it." Instead,

Amidala remains silent, and returns to her abusive husband, so that she can bear his heirs, die, and clear the stage for the "chosen one" to fight for liberty, in twenty years or so.

Perhaps Lucas has set out to make a different sort of Star Wars movie in the prequels- it may be that he wished to make a *film noir* Star Wars film. There are some superficial similarities to *film noir* in the prequels, particularly in the last two films- urban settings, art deco designs, and the dark and moody lighting effects that give "noir" its name. However, they are missing one of the classic defining elements of the genre. Roger Ebert has defined film noir as being about an innocent or everyman discovering his own capacity for evil.

Had this been handled well, Anakin's descent into evil could have been compelling and sympathetic. But from the beginning of the second film, Anakin is petulant, arrogant and egocentric. There is no gradual slide to evil, nor a catastrophic transformation- at sometime between the first and second films, Anakin has already become irredeemably evil, for little clear reason. Thus, there we do not sympathetically follow his descent, but instead merely watch it predictably unfold, alternately bored, annoyed or repulsed.

However all of these flaws that were present in the prequels are not the most important reason for their ethical and aesthetic failure. Implied in all of this critique is a comparison with the originals. To understand why the prequels failed in that comparison , we must discover what was present in the originals that made them good, and thus see its absence in the originals.

Why the Original Star Wars Movies Were Good.

The first three Star Wars episodes , that is episodes 4 through 6- (*A New Hope, The Empire Strikes Back, and Return of the Jedi*) were brilliant and important films. Their innovation lies in their syncratism, that is Lucas consciously decided to attempt to recreate the feel of movie adventure serials of his child hood. This is reflected cinematically in the exotic locations, the use of wipes for scene changes, and the use of the cliff hanger. In some cases, characters literally hang from cliffs, Han in the Sarlac Pit in *Jedi,* Luke under the city of Bespin in *Empire.* Each film also has Luke swing on a rope across some chasm, a nod to the Tarzan and pirate serials. Chewbacca even roars a version of Johnny Weismuller's famous Tarzan yodel when he swings through the trees in *Return of the Jedi.*

These serials in turn relied upon their literary forebearers, the pulp fiction series such as Doc Savage, Flash Gordon, Buck Rodgers, etc. Yet Lucas combined these styles with a richly developed new world, which while derivative of its forebears, was creative and original in its synthesis. The development of special effects technology which was good enough to contribute to and not distract from the story telling was also important to the films' success.

Star Wars is not what is referred to as 'hard science fiction', in that it does not base its story upon speculation about future technological or sociological developments that can be postulated from the current state of knowledge. It is firmly within the genre of science fiction known as "space opera" in which the science takes a back seat to the adventure. The science gives a superficial gloss to otherwise established fantasy and adventure motifs- light sabers for swords, Jedi who are both knights and wizards, the freeing of the princess from the death star rather than a castle, etc. Again, this was a conscious effort by Lucas to rely upon universal tropes, derived indirectly from Carl Jung through Joseph Campbell.

A common error in film criticism, both formal and casual, is to consider the director to be the most important creative force behind a film. Certainly in some films this is true, especially those that are both written and directed by the same person. However, focusing exclusively on the director obscures both the collaborative nature of film, and the often far more important contribution of the writer.

For example, while *Natural Born Killers* bears some of Oliver Stone's directoral touches, it has much more in common thematically with the other works of its screenwriter, Quentin Tarantino, than it does with the other works of Stone's, such as *the Doors* or *Nixon. Natural Born Killers* is a Tarantino film that happens to have been directed by someone else. Rare is the director who has the perspective or humility of Terry Gilliam, who describes his work as director on films that he has not written himself as that of "a hired hand."

It should also be noted that of the three originals, only the first, *A New Hope,* was written solely by Lucas. While Lucas contributed the story outline for episodes 5 and 6, *Empire Strikes Back* (the most critically acclaimed of the films) was written by Leigh Brackett and Lawrence Kasdan, while Kasdan has the sole writing credit for *Return of the Jedi.* These are two talented and successful screenwriters, Brackett comes from an older Hollywood lineage, having written some of the films that Lucas likely grew up watching, such as *Rio Bravo, Rio Lobo,* and *The Big Sleep,* even having collaborated with William Faulkner. Just as importantly, she was also a talented writer of science fiction, having written numerous stories in the genre. Indeed, *Empire* was her swan song, as she died in 1978, before the film was complete. Kasdan, though of a later generation, has a similarly impressive list of credits, such as *The Big Chill, Silverado,* and *Wyatt Earp.* (It is debatable how much of the finished screenplay was Brackett's, and how much Kasdan's but the point remains that it was not solely Lucas' work.) The relevance of this to Star Wars is that while Lucas wrote *A New Hope,* he did not write *Empire* or *Jedi,* but he did write all three of the prequels (with help from Johnathan Hales on *Attack of the Clones.*) In the intervening years, he lost sight of the most important idea underlying the first film.

This, the most important underlying trope within the first Star Wars trilogy is the plot of *Casablanca.* Not only is this key for understanding the moral underpinning of the first three movies, but it is the departure from this that explains the failure of the second three. The playwright Maxwell Anderson in his essay "A Faith in Theater," describes several rules necessary for a good piece of drama. Among these are:

1. The story must be of what happens within the mind and heart of a man or woman. The external events are only symbolic of what happens within.
2. The story must be a conflict between the forces of good and evil within a single person.
3. The protagonist must represent the forces of good and must win, or if he has been evil, must yield to the forces of good and know himself defeated.
4. The protagonist cannot be a perfect person. He must come out at the end a more admirable person than he went in.

While an argument can be made as to whether these rules must hold for every artistically successful film, it is clear that these must hold true for every successful Star Wars film. The "formula" of a Star Wars film is merely a specific variant of the above rules, derived from *Casablanca.* It is the departure from that formula, which I will elaborate on below, that is the greatest disappointment in the prequels.

Everyone Comes to Lando's

Star Wars shares much superficially with *Casablanca.* Luke's home planet of Tatooine, where much of the important action of *A New Hope* takes place, was actually filmed in the Tatoon dessert of North Africa, not far, globally speaking, from Morocco and the city of Casablanca. Moreover, the long establishing sequence at the beginning of *Casablanca* that introduces us to a polyglot, multi-ethnic community of desperate refugees, pickpockets and con-men is echoed in the "wretched hive of scum and villainy" of Mos Eisley Spaceport. Lucas has acknowledged that the corpulent crime lord, Jabba the Hutt, was based on *Casablanca*'s Signor Ferrari, as played by Sidney Greenstreet. The two films also share the need for the protagonists to escape the city without being detected by authoritarian forces, and share the depiction of those forces. The uniforms of the Imperial officers, the back of Darth Vader's helmet, the use of the term "Stormtroopers" and their willingness to commit genocide (the destruction of Alderran by the Death Star) were all inspired by the Nazis. (Although one should note that the Death Star's indiscriminate planet destroying power is as reminiscent of the bombing of Hiroshima and Nagasaki as it is of the concentration camps. Other parallels to American imperialism will arise in *Return of the Jedi* as well.)

However, the most important similarity between *Casablanca* and *A New Hope* is the plot and the concomitant character development of one of the main protagonists. In *Casablanca*, the plot rests on a love triangle between Rick Blaine, Ilsa Lund, his former lover and Victor Lazlo, her husband and wanted resistance leader. (This love triangle is repeated in

Star Wars with Han Solo, the scoundrel, Luke the goody two-shoes, but in a nice bit of feminism, Princess Leia is the resistance leader.) The plot is resolved when Rick has obtained the upper hand and has two letters of transit, the means of escape from the city and the Nazis, for two of the three.

Up to this point of the film Rick's moral character has been in question. He asserts that he is only looking out for himself, "I stick my neck out for nobody" and "I'm the only cause I'm interested in," and allows an associate to be killed despite his pleas for help- (Peter Lorre's now famous "You've got to help me Rick") On the other hand, he fixes a roulette game to allow a young bride to win the money for a visa, thus saving her from having to sleep with the lecherous police captain. It is also established that he had run guns to the Ethiopians fighting the Italian fascists, and fought for the Loyalists in Spain, though he claims that in both instances he was only doing it for the money. He is cynical, bitter and a hard drinker. Yet when the moment of truth arises at the climax of the film, he rediscovers his conscience, and sends Lazlo to freedom in his place. He sacrifices his own happiness for a greater cause, at the risk of his own survival, for he will remain in the still very dangerous city of Casablanca. It is a far, far better thing Rick does than he has ever done before.

This trope, of the person of questionable moral character choosing to risk their life and happiness in pursuit of the greater good at the climax of the film, is repeated four times in the first three Star Wars films, and is their source of moral and emotional power. In *A New Hope*, the Rick Blaine character is Han Solo. Despite Luke's presence as the protagonist, Luke exhibits less character growth, much of which takes place in the first half of the film. Once he decides to leave Tatooine after the death of his family, Luke is mainly swept up in the action, doing what he is expected to do as the hero. Han, a classic anti-hero, is a cynical scoundrel and rogue who is looking only out for himself. “I don't stick my neck out for anybody.” Han has joined in the rescue effort of Princess Leia only for the money, and leaves the Rebels before the climactic battle in order to use that money to pay off the debt that has placed a bounty on his head. He leaves despite Luke's pleading for him to stay and fight for something greater than himself.

Thus the moment of most excitement in the film, and that which elicits the biggest cheer from the audience, is not when Luke blows up the Death Star, but when Han, piloting the Millennium Falcon, returns to the battle of the Death Star to save Luke's life, even though he risks his own in the process. The Millennium Falcon diving into the battle, with the sun shining like a halo behind it is the most heroic and emotionally stirring moment of the film. Not to belabor the point, but as “sacrifice” literally means “ to make holy,” Han's sacrifice of the ability to pay off the price on his head earns him that halo.

A common school yard debate of 1977 was who one would rather be- Luke or Han? While Luke might be more powerful, Han was the better person.

This is similar to the perennial debate of the comic book store- Superman, or Batman? The born hero, or the self-made one? It is of note that Spiderman, in his original iteration, includes elements of both- he has greatness thrust upon him by the radioactive spider bite, yet only becomes a hero when he invents his own web-shooters and, inspired by his uncle's death, (much like Luke and his aunt and uncle, or Batman and his parents) decides to use his powers for the greater good.

In *The Empire Strikes Back*, the trope is repeated with a new scoundrel, Lando Calrissian introduced to play the role of the now reformed Han. Lando's morality is in question from his first appearance, when Han doubts his trustworthiness, and Lando greets Han, et.al. with a pretense of anger and menace. Lando moves from scoundrel to actual villain when he betrays the heroes to Darth Vader and the Empire, resulting in their capture, torture, and Han's freezing in carbonite, as well as Luke's loss of a hand. However, when things look most bleak for the heroes, Lando has a conversion of a sort as well, and frees Leia and Chewbacca, and attempts to rescue Han, even though this means he loses his ownership of Cloud City, and he must flee as a refugee. In keeping with the darker tone of the film, his attempt at saving them is only partially successful, but he does redeem himself, and becomes an active leader of the rebellion in the next film.

In *Return of the Jedi,* the final film of this trilogy, the character who redeems himself is Darth Vader. Up to this point he has been thoroughly evil, participating in the slaughter of millions, killing his subordinates, and torturing the protagonists. He has attempted to corrupt his own son and seduce him to the dark side of the Force, so that they may rule the galaxy together. However, at the climactic battle, he has apparently succeeded in exploiting Luke's anger to drive him to the Dark Side, and is then defeated physically by Luke.

But when the Emperor attempts to kill Luke, Vader's son, Vader turns against the Emperor, killing him and saving his son, but suffering fatal wounds in the process. This is the most problematic of the three conversions, in that it would seem to redeem him in the eyes of his son, and thus the audience, even though killing the emperor to save his own son doesn't seem to really make up for the slaughter of millions. It appears that the Jedi of the title who "returns" is not Luke, but Anakin.

Finally, the fourth instance of this trope taking place is best viewed by examining the three films together as one long story. By doing so, the position of Luke as protagonist of the series is more clear. In the first film, Luke is the innocent farm boy, not so subtly reflected in his white clothing. In this film, while adolescently whiny, he performs a archetypal role of the young hero. In a motif that has been repeated from Dorothy leaving grey Kansas for Oz, Frodo leaving the shire, or Harry Potter leaving the Dursleys, Luke is drawn out of his boring mundane world into one of magic and excitement, to find himself, in part because of a parental legacy, thrust into the middle of an epic battle between good and evil.

Within the first film, Luke performs this role well, if somewhat unremarkably. He does mature a bit from the beginning to the end, in part because he witnesses the deaths of his surrogate parents, his mentor, Obi-Wan, and Biggs, his childhood friend. However, as mentioned before, the more dramatic character growth in this film is Han's.

In the second film the *Empire Strikes Back*, the most emotionally rich of the three, Luke's character becomes more complex. In a vision from Obi-Wan, he is told to seek out a new teacher, Yoda. Under Yoda's teaching, Luke develops more complexity, his adolescent whining becoming impatience and immaturity, which Yoda rightly fears as dangerous. His childlike conception that Jedis should be great warriors is shown to be just that- childish. This complexity is again reflected in costuming, as Luke wears a grey outfit through most of the film.

Notably, on Dagobah Luke suffers a crisis in faith in the Force, and is unable to lift his space craft because of it. Most tellingly, during a vision quest he is sent on by Yoda, he refuses to heed Yoda's advice to leave his weapons behind, and encounters a vision of Darth Vader. He defeats the vision only to see the helmet split and his own face inside. Despite this warning that he has the potential to go over to the Dark side, he leaves Yoda to attempt to save his friends when he receives a warning that they are in danger.

He thus falls into a trap set by Vader for him, at which Vader defeats him, cutting off his hand, and then attempts to get him to join him by revealing that he is Luke's father. Luke refuses and flees, leaping into a massive pit, sliding down various tunnels, and ending up hanging underneath Bespin city, from an antenna that can be viewed as an upside down cross, among fiery colored clouds, an inverted heaven. This can be viewed as the Campbellian hero's descent into hell, and Luke's suffering and complaint to Obi-wan that he lied to Luke about his father is not dissimilar to "Eli, Eli, Lama Sabachtani."

However, one should not overly emphasize the Christ imagery here, because Luke's journey is not complete. After being saved by his friends, the last image of the film is of him being fitted with a cybernetic hand, over which he slips a black glove, both reminiscent of his father's less than human cybernetic body and Vader's black armor and costume that reflects his allegiance to the dark side.

In the last film,*Return of the Jedi,* Luke is wearing all black, in an outfit that has hints of a priest's cassock and a kung-fu shirt, evocative of the Jedi's position as warrior monks, but which also suggests Luke's descent into the dark side. In Luke's assault on Jabba's palace he chokes one of the guards with the Force in a manner we have seen performed by Vader. Han, however, remains skeptical of Luke's Jedi status, and Luke fails to use his Jedi mind powers on Jabba.

In his final fight with Vader, he cuts off his father's hand in an echo of Luke's own wounding in *The Empire Strikes Back.* To further drive home this similarity we see that Vader's hand and forearm are also cybernetic. However, when the Emperor attempts to convert Luke to the Dark Side and goads him to kill his father, Luke refuses, and throws away his light saber, now rejecting the weapon that he could not deny himself in Yoda's cave. The Emperor attempts to kill him, and Luke refuses to fight back, knowing that to do so would be to give in to the Dark Side. As previously mentioned, this stirs Vader to action, and he kills the Emperor, saving his son, though loosing his own life in the process.

However, both Luke's and Vader's sacrifices are more personal than those of Han or Lando, and do nothing much to help the rest of the galaxy. Unlike Han and Lando, Luke and Vader only save each others' lives, and this remains irrelevant to the larger struggle between the Empire and Rebels waging outside the Throne Room. The commando actions of Han, Chewbacca, Leia and the Ewoks (recruited to the cause through the translations of C-3PO) on Endor destroy the energy shield protecting the Death Star, allowing Lando, Wedge and a multi-species rebel fleet to destroy the Death Star, which presumably would have killed the Emperor, no matter the resolution of the family squabble on board. (It is also notable that critics have seen the Ewoks, and their low-tech jungle warfare defeating the Empire as suggestive of the Viet Cong, thus also making the Empire symbolic of the American Empire.)

Further, Darth Vader's conversion, while superficially similar to that of Rick, Lando, etc. is qualitatively different. The Rick archetype is one of moral ambiguity- Rick is seemingly self interested, yet he had done good in the past- running arms to Ethiopia, saving the girl from Louis, etc.

Similarly, Han and Lando are gamblers and scoundrels, with Han abandoning his friends prior to the battle of Endor, and Lando turning over Han to Vader. Yet both fight to make these errors right, and risk their own lives to do so.

Anakin/Vader on the other hand is not morally ambiguous at all. At the end of *Revenge of the Sith,* Kenobi and Yoda suggest that there is "still good in him" which serves to set up the entire six films as the story of Anakin's redemption. But whatever good that the Jedi see in him is nowhere evidenced on the screen. He is blatantly evil- more akin to Hitler than Rick. He kills subordinates on a whim, tortures Han and Princess Leia (though he is seemingly unaware that she is his own daughter) and assists in the destruction of an entire planet. Yet we are expected to accept his conversion, as if merely saving his own son is enough to make up for all the suffering he caused.

However, Vader risks nothing to save Luke, so it is hardly a sacrifice. Further, when viewed with Vader's knowledge of the workings of the Sith, as explained in the prequels, rebelling against the Emperor is Vader's only sensible move at this point and is self-serving, not selfless. There seems to be no flaw of the original trilogy that is not made worse by the prequels. For the prequels state that there are only two Sith in existence at any one time, a master and an apprentice, though why this should be is never explained. It is a strategic error on the part of the Sith to limit themselves in such a way, especially when their enemy, the Jedi, number in the hundreds and operate a large school for training new Jedi. The Sith's apparently self-imposed limit on their own numbers seems foolish for a sect bent on accumulating power and dominating the galaxy.

But such a limit also makes it clear that the only way to advance in the ranks of the Sith is to kill one's master, as it is implied that the Emperor did. Moreover, as any Sith master knows that his apprentice will eventually want to kill him, it is also in the master's self interest to kill his apprentices when they become too powerful. Anakin is aware of this from the prequels, with the Emperor's previous apprentices, Darth Maul and Count Dooku having been slain in the furtherance of Palpatine's plans. Thus, it should be obvious to Vader that at some point he must either kill the Emperor or be killed by him- and it is perhaps toward this end that he tries to recruit Luke in *The Empire Strikes Back.* So, when Vader turns against the Emperor at the end of *Return of the Jedi,* he really has nothing to lose. The Emperor has made it clear that he is willing to have Vader killed and supplanted as apprentice. His options at this point are to stand by as the Emperor kills Luke, or turn against the Emperor, and try to possibly save his own life and that of his son. Standing by and watching the Emperor kill Luke will not gain him anything- as he is clearly, and irrevocably, out of the Emperor's favor- nor will turning against the Emperor harm his position significantly. Further, he does not know when he turns on the Emperor that doing so will cost him his life. Unlike Rick, Han or Lando, he has nothing to give up or risk, nothing to sacrifice that will make his action a selfless act. Far from turning away from evil to good, Vader is really only pursuing the only course available to him, yet we are supposed to see this as a grand conversion on his part.

In the final sequence of *Return of the Jedi*, Luke sees a vision of the smiling "ghosts" of Ob-wan, Yoda, and Anakin as well- the Star Wars equivalent of apotheosis. The false distinction between Anakin and Vader serves to remove from Anakin the moral responsibility for his atrocities. Anakin is spoken of being "killed" by Vader, as if he were possessed by a demon, as if "Vader made me do it." It is noteworthy that here in *Return of the Jedi* some of the tendencies that wrecked the prequel trilogy are already beginning to emerge.

The last minute conversion of Anakin/Vader does not fit well into the Rick Blaine trope- but is does fit an American film variant of the Faustian dilemma. This is an important enough distinction to warrant further explanation.

The Three Resolutions to the Faustian Dilemma

The Classical and Renaissance Faust

The Faustian Dilemma is one of the perennial stories in Western culture with versions by Christopher Marlowe, Thomas Mann, Goethe, Liszt,

Mahler and many others. It contains the following recurring elements:

Faust himself is usually an outsider, or an outcast, and if not an actual wizard, a scholar pursuing knowledge, often the sort of knowledge that "man is not meant to know." Faust is tempted by a Mephistopheles character (not Satan himself, but one of his powerful minions) to enter into what is now called a Faustian bargain. For selling his soul, Faust receives power and knowledge, (and, especially in the American film version, material wealth.) This bargain usually involves the signing of an actual or symbolic contract, but it may also involve Faust committing some other evil acts as well, such as an act of violence, or betrayal of a friend. His temptation may also involve Faust's pursuit of an otherwise unobtainable love, like Gretchen in Goethe's Faust, or Helen of Troy in Marlowe's version.

Often Faust is given a second chance to reject or reaffirm the contract. Traditionally, this takes place after twenty four years from the signing of the original contract. The twenty four years are symbolic of the twenty four hours of a day, signifying the fleeting nature of the power Faust receives. At this point Mephistopheles offers further temptations and threats to secure Faust's reaffirmation of the contract.

Finally at some point the contract comes due, and it as this point that the most important variations in the Faustian story occur. There have traditionally been two different resolutions to the Faustian Dilemma.

The earliest versions of the story appear in the

late Classical period, during the beginnings of Christianity. In these stories, magicians with names such as Theopholis, Cyprian, Simon Magus, Faustus, Faustinius and others are able to escape the contract by turning to Christianity. They give up their magical powers, turn to a life of asceticism and prayer and are delivered from their debts by divine or saintly intervention.

In the Sixteenth Century in Germany an actual historical figure existed named Georg Faust. He was a con man and self-promoting huckster who cultivated the image of himself as a sorcerer. Indeed, since legends of a sorcerer named Faust were already centuries old at this point, it was likely that he took the last name of Faust to add to his mystique.

According to legend, when his contract came due he met his end in an inn near Wittenberg, and was rent limb from limb by demons. Several folk tales and published works in the era's new genre of *Teufelsbücher* (devil books) retold this story, and it served as the inspiration for Marlowe's stage version, written around 1590. In these Sixteenth Century versions of the tale, the ending is almost invariably one of punishment. No matter how remorseful Faust is, the contract cannot be broken, and he is consumed body and soul by the Devil.

It is important to note that these two versions of the Faustian story served two different functions, addressing the concerns of their times. In the Late Classical period Christianity is still a new religion, and is seeking to make converts among the pagans, the mainstream religion of the day. Thus Faust's sin of seeking knowledge, as well as the debaucheries this leads him to are symbolic of Greek philosophy and Roman hedonism. The message to the potential convert is that no matter what sins they may have committed prior to conversion, like Faust all will be forgiven if they renounce those past actions and live a clean life from now on.

By the Sixteenth Century, Christianity is now the mainstream religion in Europe and is facing outside challenges of its own, both with the turmoil of the Protestant Reformation questioning dogma, and Humanist scholarship threatening the hegemony of religion entirely. It noteworthy that Wittenberg, the site of Faust's bloody death was also the location of Germany's first secular university.

Thus, the Renaissance Faust tale is a cautionary one- Christianity is not looking to gain converts from sinners, but is seeking to keep the already believing populace from going astray. Thus, the anti-intellectual spin of the narrative encourages obedience to a given dogma, not curiosity. Both Protestants and Catholics will tell versions suggesting that is was the Pope, or Luther, respectively, that contributed to Faust being led astray.

The American Faust

Yet, there is a third option for the resolution of the Faustian Dilemma that has a particularly American character. The archetypical version of this is the short story *The Devil and Daniel Webster* written by Stephen

Vincent Benet in 1937. While Benet acknowledged the influence of an earlier Washington Irving story, *The Devil and Tom Walker,* written in 1824, Irving's story follows the traditional, Sixteenth Century resolution, and thus is not the first of what I will call "American Fausts."

In Benet's story, Jabez Stone, a New Hampshire farmer, has entered into a bargain with "Old Scratch" for wealth and a prosperous farm. When the contract comes due, however, he seeks the assistance of famed lawyer, orator and Senator, Daniel Webster. Webster is able to get the soul back from Satan by asking for a trial of his peers. The devil complies, assembling a jury of dead notorious American sinners. By the force of his oratory, Webster is able to sway the emotions of the jaded, damned jury members, who rule in Webster's favor, in an example of jury nullification.

This is part of the American folk tradition of the tall tale- that Davy Crockett was such a good shot he could hit one bullet with another, that Pecos Bill could break and ride a tornado, etc. Thus, Daniel Webster was such a good orator that he could talk a soul away from the devil.

But it also begins a variation of the Faustian tale in which one can escape the Devil's bargain by trickery or besting him at some feat- be it courtroom oratory, or fiddle playing, as in Charlie Daniel's 1979 song, *The Devil went Down to Georgia.* (Coincidentally, Daniels has cited a 1925 poem of Benet's *The Mountain Whippoorwill,* which describes a fiddle contest, as his inspiration for this song.)

This is the morality of the American get-rich-quick scheme, not the Puritan work ethic- not only does the Faust character not have to repent, but he gets to keep the fiddle of gold, or the prosperous farm. We are a nation of Captain Kirks, who don't believe in a no-win scenario, confident that we can pull a clever trick out of our sleeve to save our skins, or souls, at the last minute. This should be distinguished from the Classical Faust, because even in versions where the protagonist repudiates the contract and thus regains his soul, the American Faust still gets to keep whatever he sold his soul for.

For example, In *Damn Yankees,* the stage musical of 1955 and its film versions, when the protagonist who has sold his soul to play professional baseball gives up his devil-granted prowess in order to keep his soul, he is still able to hit a home run against the Yankees, (keeping the girl and the glory,) despite reverting to his pre-contract amateur self.

Further, the 2000 American remake of the 1967 British film *Bedazzled* is altered such that the Faust character is spared by a selfless act, and while not getting his original Gretchen character, ends up with an even better girl.

By the late twentieth century, especially in the medium of film, an additional, ominous element was added. Rather than merely besting Satan at some competition, redemption could be achieved by killing the Devil. I will examine three of these – *The Little Mermaid, Little Shop of Horrors,* and *Heathers* in depth.

In 1989's *The Little Mermaid*, Faust is Ariel, the title character. She is a scholar of sorts, in that she collects artifacts of the surface world, and speculates about their function, but she is also a materialistic collector who sings of wanting more.

She is also in love with a human, Prince Eric, her "Gretchen" figure. In order to gain legs, so that she can court her love, and experience the surface world, she sells her voice to Ursula the Sea Witch. The deal is signed in a song "Poor Unfortunate Souls" which is rife with Faustian imagery including the signing of a literal contract. Because of this deal, she puts not only her soul, but the entire underwater kingdom of her father, Triton at risk.

Ariel escapes her contract, but only because a male surrogate, Prince Eric, kills the Sea Witch for her. Indeed, this film, like much Disney fare, is extremely sexist and anti-sexuality. Ariel's sin is to seek control of her own sexuality (her "legs") and worse, she does so through consulting with another woman. She seeks to leave the sea when her father discovers her pining over a statue of the Prince, and in a rage, he destroys the statue. This emasculates her father- Ariel's escape from her father's control enables Ursula to steal Triton's trident and magically transform him into an atrophied wisp. It is only when another male, Prince Eric, kills Ursula by driving the prow of a ship into her ample chest that order is restored. Now that the prince has proved his loyalty to social order and male control of female sexuality by slaying a rogue woman, he has redeemed himself in Triton's sight. Triton consents to the marriage of Prince Eric and Ariel, at a ceremony where control of her is passed from one male to another. With a wave of his magical trident, Triton bestows legs on Ariel, thus affirming that the two lovers were not separated by the sea, but merely by lack of paternal approval- presumably, Triton could have granted her wish at the beginning.

But through an act of violence, even if only that of a surrogate, Ariel is able to escape the contract, suffer no punishment for endangering the kingdom, and get the reward that she sold herself for- to be part of the Prince's world, in a elaborate and luxurious wedding ceremony.

In *Little Shop of Horrors*, (1986) the Faust character is Seymour Krelborn. His last name is a reference to the Krels, the alien race in the film *Forbidden Planet* (1956) who destroy themselves by their research into forbidden science. This is but one of many examples of the complex interconnection between the Faust and Frankenstein myths. *Forbidden Planet* is itself an adaptation of Shakespeare's *The Tempest* in which a somewhat Faustian sorcerer, Prospero, must forsake his magic before he can rejoin society.

Seymour lives in abject poverty, which he sings about in the song “Skid Row” where he foreshadows his Faustian bargain with the lyric “I'd do I don't know what to get out of Skid Row.” Seymour is also an amateur scholar/scientist in that “rare and unusual plants” are his hobby. One such plant, Audrey

II, named for his unrequited love, Audrey, (another Gretchen figure) a co-worker of his at Mushkin's flower shop, is the Mephistopheles character. Audrey II is actually a sentient, alien life-form with magic powers.

Audrey II tempts Seymour with offers of wealth and power, including the ability to win over Audrey. However, the price is that the plant, reminiscent of a giant Venus Fly-trap, must be fed blood, and eventually even human sacrifices. Seymour balks at this initially, but he ultimately gives in, killing Audrey's abusive boyfriend and feeding him to the plant. When discovered at this by Mushkin, the flower store owner and surrogate father, Seymour kills him as well.

The second temptation occurs in the song "The Meek Shall Inherit" in which Seymour receives offers for television and book contracts. He sings "I take these offers, it means more killings/Who knew success would come with messy nasty strings?/I sign these contracts/It means I'm willing/to keep on doing bloody awful evil things" He has resolved that the "vegetable must be destoyed," when he realizes that doing so might lose him his love Audrey. "Without my plant/she might not love me anymore." He gives in, signing the contracts, signing away his soul.

But when the plant tries to eat Audrey, Seymour attacks the plant, destroying it by electrocution. Seymour and Audrey get a happy ending, in their longed for "Somewhere That's Green"

In the film *Heathers* (1988) the protagonist, a

high school girl named Veronica enters the Faustian contract twice. Her first bargain is with the Heathers, the most popular clique in school, three girls all named Heather, referred to by number. She is a scholar of sorts, in that much of the narration is in the form of her diary entries. Manipulations of letters, petitions, and signatures, as well as flame imagery, figure heavily throughout the film,

She describes the Heathers as co-workers that she does not like very much, and their job is being popular. In carrying out this "job" Veronica forges a note from a popular jock to an unpopular, overweight girl Martha "Dumptruck" Dunstock, resulting in Martha's public humiliation. Her contract comes due, however, when Heather #1 expects Veronica to sleep with one of her college friends. When Veronica refuses, Heather #1 threatens her with social ostracism, a trash can flaming symbolically in the background.

However, to escape from this "hell", Veronica enters into a second pact with a different Mephistopheles- the dangerous new kid in town, JD. He tricks her into helping him kill Heather #1, and Veronica forges a suicide note from Heather to cover it up. JD leads her into further violence, including two more deaths and forged suicide notes. Finally Veronica fakes her own death to escape JD's influence and discovers that JD has tricked her and everyone else in the school into signing a mass suicide note, and he plans on blowing up the school during a pep rally, killing everyone. Veronica confronts and shoots JD, fatally wounding him and saving the lives of everyone in the school.

What is particularly notable about these three versions of the American Faustian dilemma is that they were all changed when made into film. Hans Christian Anderson's original 1837 Little Mermaid story doesn't easily fit the Faust model. The sea witch is a less malevolent figure, and the mermaid trades her voice for legs, but not her soul. The sea witch even assists the Little Mermaid's sisters in trying to save her after the Prince betrays her. The Little Mermaid does not have to destroy her or get out of a contract. When given a choice of killing the prince who has broken her heart so that she can become a mermaid again, she chooses to die instead- though this sacrifice results in her becoming an angelic "daughter of the air."

The 1986 film version of *Little Shop of Horrors* was an adaptation of the 1982 stage musical of the same name, that was itself based on an old black and white low-budget non-musical film from 1960. In the stage show, however, the ending is also the traditional Renaissance ending- Seymour's attack on the plant fails, he and Audrey are both eaten, and the chorus sings the moral of the story "They may offer you fortune and fame/cars and money and instant acclaim/but no matter whatever they offer you/don't feed the plants/." However, when this ending was filmed for the movie and shown to test audiences, they responded poorly and the new, happy, "Hollywood" ending was written and shot.

The original screenplay of Heathers ended with JD blowing up the school, killing himself and

Veronica. The final scene would be various characters, popular and unpopular dancing together at a prom in the afterlife- for as JD says earlier in the film "The only place that different social classes can get along is in heaven."

By allowing Heather to kill JD and escape any repercussions for the three murders she has helped commit, the film reiterates the American Faust. This is particularly disappointing in that it also enervates the social critique inherent in the film. JD says the the school "self-destructs not because society didn't care, but because high school was society." Veronica is horrified to realize that after killing Heather #1, the new head of the clique, Heather #2, previously bullied, becomes a bully just as mean. Power is absolutely corrupting.

But in the filmed ending, Veronica takes Heather #1's red hair scrunchy, (symbolic of the crown of social leadership) from Heather #2, and puts it on her own head, saying "There's a new sheriff in town." She then asks Martha Dumptruck over to watch movies. Thus, the critique of the social structure is de-fanged- it's not the position that is wrong, just the individuals that happen to hold it. Once the "bad apples" are expunged, a benevolent dictator can take over, and all will be right with the world.

All three of these in their original versions were variations on the Renaissance Faust- the Faust character cannot escape the bargain, and is punished for giving into temptation. But in their modified film iterations, the Fausts can escape, and keep the wealth and power that they have sold their souls for by resorting to violence. Not only does this regain their souls, but it absolves them of guilt for the murders that they will have committed to gain that wealth and power.

Without belaboring the point I will mention that many other American films, such as the *Witches of Eastwick,* follow this same pattern. In its adaptation from John Updike's 1982 novel, the 1986 film version is heavily altered, better fitting the American Faust pattern. The titular witches violently destroy the devil character, yet get to keep his mansion and live happily ever after- not the ending of the novel.

It is an interesting commentary on American film audiences, or at least the perception of those audiences by filmmakers, that the traditional Faust resolutions are acceptable in stage plays, novels, fairy tales and foreign film, but are not acceptable as Hollywood movies. In this venue, and time period, only the American Faust resolution is presentable. It should be noted that the time period of the greatest manifestation of the American Faust trope- the 1980's and 1990's- is a period of re-militarization, jingoism and the rejection of the self-critique of the Civil Rights and Vietnam eras -Reagan's “Morning in America” up to the “Early Afternoon” of the Second Bush Administration. This is also the period book-ended by the two sets of Star Wars films.

Darth Faust

Lucas has included the American Faust trope

in the Star Wars films. It occurs twice, once with Luke as Faust, once with Anakin. Luke is himself tempted twice, once by his father, Darth Vader, as Mephistopheles in *Empire Strikes Back,* and once by the Emperor in *Return of the Jedi.* In both cases, Luke rightfully refuses the temptation to sell his soul and join the Dark Side, even if it means his own death. He leaps to what might possibly be his death in *Empire* rather than join Vader, and he throws away his sword, rather than join the Emperor in *Jedi*.

Luke's action is compatible with both the Classical and Renaissance Faust, because in either the best option would be not to enter into the pact to begin with. However, Anakin's actions viewed throughout the six films in their entirety follows the trope of the American Faust. Born a poor slave, but with a scholar's interest in robotics and spaceflight, he studies magic only to be tempted by the Mephistophelian Emperor. He finally gives in to the Dark Side to win the love and life of his Gretchen, Amidala, even though it means the eventual death of millions.

By viewing the six films in the context of the American Faust, it becomes clear that Anakin's redemption and apotheosis at the end of *Return of the Jedi,* is not so much because he turns from the Dark Side, nor even that he saves the life of his son- after all one life hardly makes up for millions. No, he, like Seymour, Ariel and Veronica, is absolved by violence. Since the Devil made him do it, and he has killed that devil, then no one is to blame, and all is forgotten and forgiven.

But more so than the inclusion of the American Faust, (which doesn't reach its fruition until *Return of the Jedi*) what most impoverishes the prequel trilogy is that Lucas has forgotten the Rick Blaine trope. There is no hero in this sense in any of the three prequel movies. At no point is there a conversion moment, like Han returning to battle, or Lando switching sides for the audience to cheer on. There is not even a moment of Luke throwing away his sword. There is no moral suspense, no moral choice. In *Empire,* Lando, in trying to justify his betrayal of his friends, claims "I had no choice." He later disproves this when he chooses to side with the good, even though he loses his wealth and status by doing so.

In the prequels, no one chooses to be good or evil, they are merely assigned to a team from the beginning by Lucas. The evil are cartoonishly so, and the good are wooden, "good" merely because that is the team to which they have been assigned.

Why it Matters

Putting aside the trivial annoyances- Jar-Jar, the midichlorins, why does is matter that Lucas failed so spectacularly? That can be answered by looking at the mythic component of the films. In this case I refer to mythic in the Jungian/Campbellian sense, of a epic whose purpose is not only to entertain, but to pass on the collective moral vision of the culture. What is the moral of the Star Wars films?

As should be obvious by now, as the morality of the films changes drastically between the two sets of films. In the originals, there are clear cut good and evil actions, though people may be morally complex. In the prequels, there are no clear cut good and evil actions, yet people are simplistic.

The change in morality between the two films can be read as a reflection of the changes in political and ethical debate in the United States in the over twenty years between the release of the first film and the first of the prequels.

The original trilogy began at the end of the Seventies, when the successes of the civil rights movements and the end of the Vietnam war were fresh in people's minds. Civil rights were good, napalming children was bad, and intelligent people were confident they could tell the difference.

After the Eighties and Nineties, the nation's ethical discourse had changed. 'Morality' had been largely abandoned to the evangelical Right's prurient obsessions with who was putting what where in the bedroom. The intellectual moderate left had been seduced by the facile arguments of post-modernism and had abandoned the notion of absolute truth and morality altogether. Moral, ethical and epistemological relativism ruled the day. Evil was no longer wrong, it was merely "problematic" and the only universal sin was insisting that there was some universal standards of right and wrong.

By the prequels, this type of thought had made its way into Lucas's thinking, consciously or not. In the opening crawl for *Attack of the Clones* Lucas states that there are good people fighting on both sides of the war, and that there is evil everywhere. In *Revenge of the Sith,* during the climactic confrontation between Anakin and Obi-wan, Obi- wan explicitly denies any sort of absolute truth, and thus any basis for morality when he states that "Only the Sith deal in absolutes." He implies without giving any reason that such absolute belief is wrong.

It is simple, but worthwhile, to point out that this is an absurd statement- for Obi-wan's statement, and it's implication "dealing in absolutes is wrong" are themselves absolute statements. This is the logical poverty behind all such morally relativistic schemes. It is absurd to assert that saying that slavery, torture, and genocide are absolutely wrong is itself (absolutely) wrong, yet that is what Lucas would have us believe. So much for the Jedi bringing justice to the galaxy, for of course, "justice" is an absolute concept.

Further Obi-wan argues that "Good is a point of view, Anakin. The Sith and the Jedi are similar in almost every way, including their quest for greater power." The logical consequence of moral relativism is nihilism, and whether this was Lucas' conscious intent, he has created nihilistic films in the prequels. The personal passivity of his characters, who cannot escape their roles and must only watch evil unfold, is matched by the philosophical passivity of Lucas himself when he denies that good and evil exist.

Moral complexity is not the same thing as moral confusion. Lucas wants to have it both ways- in that he argues that there is no inherent good and evil, and that in the Clone wars there is evil on all sides.

Yet, the bulk of the adversaries of the Republic army are battle droids. It is a common device in science fiction to have the role of the enemy be filled by killer robots or insectoid aliens (such as in *Starship Troopers*, amongst many others.) This allows one to engage in adolescent power fantasies of waging war, without the moral responsibility of taking actual human lives. Thus all the excitement of warfare- battles and explosions, can be fought bloodlessly.

This trope reached its most ridiculous level in the G.I. Joe cartoons of the 1980's. Despite being about the US military, and showcasing extremely powerful weaponry, the Joes never actually killed anyone- even using the ridiculous obligatory parachute. Whenever the Joes shot down an enemy aircraft, a small parachute had to appear from the exploding plane, even whole formations worth, to establish that no person was actually being killed.

For Lucas to cast one side almost entirely as Droids, and who thus can be killed with impunity, cast doubt on his contention that there are heroes and evil on both sides of the conflict. Apparently for Lucas, not all evil is really evil. This is quite different from the original trilogy, in which characters that we care about- Uncle Owen, Aunt Beru, Biggs, etc.- are killed, others, Leia, Han, Chewbacca, are tortured, showing the seriousness of the evil of the Empire, and that wars result in real deaths. The violence of the prequels is sanitized by its computer generated anonymity, and by Lucas' aforementioned assertion, against all offered evidence, that Droids cannot think, and therefore their deaths are meaningless.

To put it simply,

The morality of the original trilogy:

1. Good and Evil exist
2. Evil is tempting, but ultimately weaker than good.
3. People have free will and can choose to be good.
4. Even morally ambiguous or conflicted characters can choose to be good.
5. Good can triumph over evil

The morality of the prequel trilogy:

1. Good and Evil are ambiguous.
2. Clarity of vision on good and evil is itself evil, and thus parodoxically non-existent.
3. Power is a matter of inherent inborn elitism
4. Events are predestined, free will is weak at best
5. The morally good or ambiguous are powerless to stop evil

Further, when the six films are taken together as one massive story arc, a final set of moral principles is articulated.

1. The deathbed conversion of one evil elitist is more important than the noble sacrifice of the many good characters.
2. The evil elitist saving his own son's life, and killing his tempter, absolves him of the culpability for slaying millions, and makes him a hero.

   (This analysis is closely related to a previous

critique, as articulated by science fiction author David Brin. In an article titled *Star Wars Elitism vs. Star Trek's Populism,* Brin argues for the superiority of Star Trek over Star Wars. Star Trek, like much of hard science fiction, celebrates the collective activity that is science, and its ability to better the lives of the populace as a whole. Star Wars, like much fantasy fiction, such as the *Lord of the Rings*, and *Harry Potter*, praises the exploits of an aristocratic Übermensch, who has access to secret, esoteric powers that are inaccessible to the mases. Though, in defense of *Harry Potter*, in the final book in the series, it is not Harry Potter, the anointed one "the Boy Who Lived" who is the hero, but a Rick Blaine-style character.)

Lucas has explicitly acknowledged the influence of Joseph Campbell's 'momomyth,' as articulated in his *Hero with a Thousand Faces.* In Campbell's own words, in the monomyth "A hero ventures forth from the world of common day into a region of supernatural wonder: fabulous forces are there encountered and a decisive victory is won: the hero comes back from this mysterious adventure with the power to bestow boons on his fellow man"

While Campbell documents the prolific occurrence of the monomyth throughout world culture, is is a poverty of imagination to view this as the only possible myth, or to not locate this tradition with its historical and social context. The monomyth owes much of its ubiquity to its function in lauding powerful elites. Court jesters and story tellers quickly learn on which side their bread is buttered, and so they construct stories that justify the rule of kings and emperors. Even Shakespeare wrote history plays that ultimately served to justify the rule of the English monarchy and praise the ancestors of the current dynasty.

It has been said that is is the purpose of a writer to "comfort the afflicted, and afflict the comfortable." (This quote, originally from Finley Peter Dunne and taken out of context, has been appropriated and misattributed many times since.) This is the simple distinction between the tales of Robin Hood robbing from the rich and giving to the poor, and those praising the monarch King Arthur, though revisionist versions of the Robin Hood story even modify the tale such that Robin Hood is a benevolent noble in disguise, fighting to restore the rightful king. Many writers and artists have discovered that it is far more lucrative and beneficial to their social status to comfort the comfortable instead, to tell the nobility that they are "noble" and deserve their position of privilege. It is this end that the monomyth serves.

A noteworthy exception to this tendency in recent fantasy is the *Bartimeaus Trilogy* by Johnathan Stroud. It begins with the usual youth who is discovered to have magical powers, and is taken from his parents to be raised by wizards and schooled in magic. However, in these books the wizards openly rule a dystopian, Dickensian London, and mundane, non-magical revolutionaries fight to steal their magic and overthrow the elitist wizards. Further, it is revealed that the only source of the magician's power is demons whom the wizards summon and exploit.

Similarly, the *Matrix,* while an awful film, tempers its messianic elitism with a dose of (possibly unintended) Marxism. Neo, the messiah figure escapes the false consciousness of the Matrix and achieves (metaphorical) class consciousness- humanity (the proletariat) are exploited by the sentient machines (the bourgeoisie) and the world that humans think they inhabit is merely an illusion to mask that exploitation. Yet this same theme of unmasking false consciousness is dealt with much better, and with far less pretension, in the film *They Live.* (And yes, that film's star, professional wrestler "Rowdy" Roddy Piper, turns in a better performance than Keanu Reeves.).

However, I must respectfully disagree with Brin in his rejection of Star Wars in total, though I agree with him as regards the prequels. When viewed through the lens of the Rick Blaine *Casablanca* trope, it becomes clear that Luke, the aristocrat, is not the hero of *A New Hope,* nor *The Empire Strikes Back.* The heroes of these two films are not the elitist Jedi, but the scoundrels, Han and Lando.

To return to Maxwell Anderson's argument about the rules of drama, he makes two further points relevant to our discussion. One, he states that "excellence on stage is always moral excellence. A struggle on the part of a hero to better his material circumstances is of no interest unless his character is somehow tried in fight and comes out of the trial a better man." Merely being the best fighter pilot in the galaxy is of no inherent interest.

Lucas understood this instinctively in his script for the first Star Wars. At the climactic moment, Luke cannot merely pull the trigger and destroy the Death Star, he must first let go and trust the Force before he can succeed. Yet in the prequels, no character shows moral excellence, and the only "excellence" exhibited by Anakin is that he has more midichlorians than anyone else.

My Heretical 'Alternate Ending' to the Star Wars Saga.

The climax of the *Return of the Jedi* is two-fold. The rebels plan an attack on the second Death Star, attempting to destroy it before it becomes operational and can be used to annihilate planets, as its predecessor did in *A New Hope.* In order to do so, a commando team led by Han and Leia must take out the shield generator on the planet Endor which protects the Death Star from attack. Simultaneously, a battle fleet lead by Admiral Akbar, and a fighter squadron lead by Wedge Antilles and Lando Calrission will attack the Death Star.

Meanwhile, Luke leaves his companions and visits the Death Star to confront his father, Darth Vader, and the Emperor. Luke attempts to win his father back from the Dark Side, and engages in a lightsaber battle with him. Luke wins, cutting off Vader's hand, but refuses to kill his defeated opponent when goaded to do so by the Emperor. He nobly refuses to kill his father- noble in both the sense of honorable, but also in the aristocratic sense. For Luke is no pacifist, he has killed numerous Imperial soldiers up to this point, but he is unable to kill his own father, out of elitist loyalty, perhaps even though by any objective measure the galaxy would be far better off were Vader dead.

Luke's surrender at the end of *Return of the Jedi* is generally interpreted to be motivated by his desire to avoid giving in to the Dark Side, as if patricide is some how a “darker” crime than killing the dozens of other people he has throughout these films. Vader certainly deserves to die more so, and the galaxy would be better off without him, than say, any of the faceless stormtroopers Luke kills. Perhaps instead his surrender could be interpreted more as a suicide attempt, in that he realizes he is too weak to resist the Dark Side, and that the galaxy would be better off without another mass murder like his father running about.

The Emperor then attempts to kill Luke, as Luke will not join him. At this point Vader's conscience is awoken, and he saves Luke by killing the Emperor, though he is fatally wounded by doing so. Vader and Luke have a tearful reconciliation, and then Luke escapes with Vader's body just before the Death Star is destroyed, as the rebels, with the help of the Viet Cong-like Ewoks, have succeeded at their plan.

Luke then burns Vader's body on a funeral pyre, and the film ends with Luke seeing a vision of Obi-wan, Yoda, and Anakin happily reunited in the afterlife.

Here is my heretical, alternate ending- which

could be easily accomplished through editing the existing film. What would it matter what happens on the Death Star between Luke, Vader and the Emperor? Let us imagine that Luke does kill Vader and joins the Emperor, or the Emperor kills Luke and Vader remains loyal. The Emperor sets up a false dichotomy for Luke- that he kill his father and join the Dark Side, or he allow himself to be killed. Luke unthinkingly buys into this choice, and says he will never join the Emperor, turns off his lightsaber, and submits to be killed. More sensibly, Luke should kill his father, and then kill the Emperor. Perhaps he would be defeated, but if the Jedi are truly out to bring peace and justice to the galaxy, attempting to kill a tyrannical war monger would seem a wise choice.

Let's suppose that Luke takes this last choice, summons the emotional strength to put his murderous sadistic father down like the mad dog he is, and then turns on the Emperor. Let us further imagine that they are locked in a fierce battle, two sides of the Force "balanced." Chewbacca and the rebels take down the shield, and Lando and Wedge blow up the Death Star, killing both Luke and the Emperor. The End. Roll Credits.

This is not merely an exercise in revisionist fan fiction, but serves to demonstrate just how profoundly the prequels changed the nature of the Star Wars universe. Had only episodes 4-6 existed, then my ending would have been a tragic one, as Luke's death would have killed the last Jedi, finally extinguishing the light of the order that "brought peace and justice" to the galaxy.

Following the prequels, however, this is the most satisfying ending. For the Jedi of the prequels are elitists, who support a slave holding, tyrannical republic (an Empire in all but name), and are responsible for the creation of Vader, the clone army which becomes the Imperial Stormtroopers, and the Sith themselves. It is a common flaw for poorly thought out movies to have "bad movie math"- for example, a rescue mission that results in the deaths of more rescuers than the number of people who are successfully rescued- thus it would have been a better outcome to not stage the rescue at all. Similar is the superhero who must become a hero primarily to defeat a villain of his own creation- in which case the world would have been better had the hero never existed.

The Star Wars galaxy would have been better had Obi-Wan, and by extension, the Jedi, never existed. It takes a lot of peace and justice to make up for destroying a planet, and we see none of this in the prequels. Better that the Last Sith and the Last Jedi kill each other and be destroyed along with the Death Star. A plague on both their houses. Let the multi-ethnic, multi-gender, multi-species democratic populist rebel alliance construct a new republic, and let the Sith and the Jedi with their medieval elitism disappear.

So What?

I have argued so far that film and pop culture are a means of articulating ethical beliefs. If, as I contend, that these films may shape ethical beliefs and behavior, it would seem imperative to look for examples. As such I will look at the political impact of these films, because at their heart, politics are a public expression of our ethical beliefs. What we argue for in the public arena is an expression of our priorities and concerns as citizens and human beings. Politics, by definition being public, are also more readily apparent examples of ethical behavior than any of people's ethical behavior in more private spheres. Art can both reflect or contest existing ethical ideas, and these artistic portrayals can help legitimize those actions.

For example, the American Faust trope has implications for American politics and foreign policy. At the same time that Faustian stories were being modified to fit into the American trope for films, America fought a series of wars that also fit this trope. America enters into a Faustian pact by giving material support to a dictator or terrorist in order to gain material and strategic advantage. When this contract comes due when the devil of our creation does something of which we disapprove, we can absolve ourselves of guilt for creating that monster by slaying it.

Manuel Noriega was a paid CIA asset, even though the agency knew he was involved in drug trafficking. But by invading his country, killing thousands, and placing him under arrest, we absolve our selves of responsibility for his crimes.

Saddam Hussein was supported and armed by the US in his war against Iran, even though we knew he was a brutal dictator who would use such support to shore up his own criminal regime. The contract comes due however, when he invades Kuwait. But by killing him and destroying his government, our role in supporting him is swept under the rug. The band *They Might Be Giants* have a great lyric “You can't shake the Devil's hand and then say you are only kidding.” Unfortunately, Donald Rumsfeld has proven them wrong. Rumsfeld was photographed shaking Hussein's hand when, as part of the Reagan administration, the US supported Hussein. Yet we are supposed to forgive Rumsfeld this support because of his role in later killing Hussein.

Osama Bin Laden and his terrorist network were financed by the US government to fight against the Soviets in Afghanistan. When his Faustian contract comes due by his attack on US interests, again complicity with the devil on our part is absolved by resorting to extreme violence.

I am not arguing simplistically that this trope is the only reason that these wars were fought- there are multiple complex reasons for all of these. I am not even arguing that these are necessarily accurate depictions of the historical events- merely the public perception of them. I am arguing however, that this trope accounts for the acceptability of these wars, and lack of accountability on the part of the US government for propping up these monsters to begin with.

Politics are also a relevant consideration when evaluating the Star Wars films in that Lucas has both injected himself personally into the political sphere, as all citizens should, and because he has also injected political themes into the prequels, as I will describe below.

Darth Cheney

There are two quotes in the Revenge of the Sith that suggest Lucas intends the rise of the Emperor, Darth Vader, and the transformation of the Republic to be metaphors for the strengthening of the Imperial presidency during the Bush administration. In response to attacks from the Separatists, Palpatine seizes greater power, establishing a Galactic Empire and himself as Emperor. When the Senate votes him these powers, Amidala gives the aforementioned quote "So this is how liberty dies...with thunderous applause."

Many dictators have used external attacks as an excuse to seize power. For example Hitler used the Reichstag fire to push through emergency powers for himself, and staged the Gleiwitz incident (a faux Polish invasion of Germany, in 1939, complete with German soldiers dressed in Polish uniforms and broadcasting fake Polish propaganda) to justify invading Poland.

Another example, perhaps most analogous to Emperor Palpatine's actions, is the attack on the Roman Port of Ostia in 68 BC. Pirates attacked and burned the port city, killing many Roman citizens and capturing two senators. In response, Pompey the Great rammed through the Lex Gabinia, giving himself near dictatorial power. He did not relinquish power after destroying the pirates, but went on to conquer provinces and enrich himself, paving the way for the Emperors to come and the destruction of the Roman Republic.

(Lucas may also have intended Palapatine's destruction of the Jedi to be similar to King Philip the IV of France's destruction of the Knights Templar in 1307. Palapatine's order to simultaneously attack all Jedi is "Order 66" one digit less than the biblical "Number of the Beast" -666- while the order to kill the Templars was carried out on the now numerically infamous "Friday the 13th." Or perhaps Lucas was referencing FDR's Executive Order 9066, which authorized the Japanese Internment.")

It also appears that Lucas sees the events of Palpatine's rise to power as analogous to the irrational and disproportionate U.S. response to the terrorist attacks of September 11th. Using an outside threats as an excuse for a power grab is not exclusive to the Bush administration. Yet, there is another scene that makes the analogy to Bush more explicit. During their climactic confrontation, Anakin tells Obi-wan, in a near direct quote of Bush, "If you are not with me, you are against me."

Unfortunately, the various artistic and philosophical flaws in the film prevent this from being inspirational for political action against the War on Terror. Because the films are hobbled in their role as prologue, Amidala can merely passively observe the death of liberty, and is prevented from taking up arms against these troubles. Similarly, Obi-wan's response to Anakin- "Only the Sith deal in absolutes"- is less than a rousing call to action.

First, this is not consistent with Obi-wan's own stance- immediately prior in the conversation, Obi-wan had insisted in absolutist terms that the Sith and the Dark Side were evil. Second, while Anakin may be excluding the middle, this is hardly the greatest problem with his stance, (or Bush's, for that matter) - it is what he is arguing for- dictatorship- that is the much greater problem than his mere denial of neutrality. (Indeed, sociologists have pointed at various moments in history as “radical conversion” moments in which continued extremism create such political tensions as to prevent neutrality, and drive political actors to take sides- the use of fire hoses and dogs on civil rights workers, for example.)

But Obi-wan's philosophical inconsistency is true of the Jedi throughout the prequels. In the same conversation, he bemoans that Anakin was falsely believed to be the Chosen One, who would both “destroy the Sith” and restore “balance to the Force.” If the Jedi are the Light side, and the Sith the Dark, destroying the Sith would not balance the Force, but tilt it toward the good. But this is the philosophical muddle Lucas has talked himself into. He has lost sight of the most basic precepts of any ethical system- taking sides is not necessarily evil, not all beliefs deserve equal consideration, and in order to fight evil, some times one must take sides.

(Lucas' valorization of “Balance” is particularly ominous in the current political climate, as “balance” is the favorite rhetorical device of authoritarians who seek to undermine human rights and civil liberties- e.g. by proposing a "balance" between liberty and security. While such language appeals to careless thinkers with its false veneer of moderation, it demotes liberties from inherent rights to revocable privileges, and is directly contradicted by the absolutist language of the Bill of Rights, and has no valid place in the political discourse of a free people.)

Further, Lucas' indictment by analogy of the Bush administration in comparing them to the Empire rings a little hollow in light of the sanitizing of the violence in the prequels. One of the strongest criticisms of the Bush/Cheney administration was for its embrace of torture. Surprisingly, there is no torture evidenced in the Clone Wars trilogy. This is particularly surprising in that there is plenty of torture in the original trilogy. Darth Vader tortures Leia personally in *A New Hope,* and orders the torture of Han and Chewbacca in *Empire.* Even a droid is tortured in Jabba's palace in *Return of the Jedi.* These events show the heroism of the protagonists in withstanding these horrors, and the sheer evil of Vader and Jabba. Yet, there are no true heroes in the prequels, and since evil is "everywhere," there is no point in distinguishing one group as more evil than another.

Perhaps Lucas was less comfortable depicting torture in fiction as actual torture had most recently been thrust into the national consciousness. But such squeamishness does not serve his critique well, making it merely half-hearted.

(There are also suggestions that Lucas may have being making a comment about economics in the prequels as well. The enemies in *Phantom Menace* are the Trade Federation, whose blockade may be seen as analogous to the World Trade Organization, the World Bank and the International Monetary Fund forcing free markets on developing countries. Further, though this is a minor point in the film, Palpatine's flag ship is named *The Invisible Hand.* This phrase comes from Adam Smith's economic treatise *On the Wealth of Nations*. Smith describes the self-correcting nature of the free market as "an invisible hand" that because of competition and the laws of supply and demand, will bring prices to a moderate level. Unsophisticated readers have interpreted this to mean that a free market is the ideal system and thus should not be regulated, though Smith himself was well aware that these "corrections" could be disastrous, and though invisible, the market's hand is not a gentle one.

However, if Lucas intends an articulate economic critique in this, it is obscured by the films convoluted plot and moral relativism- after all there are "heroes" on both sides, presumably including the side of the Trade Federation.)

Barack Skywalker

Lucas has been quoted as saying that he is in favor of a benevolent dictatorship. In his support for the Obama campaign it appears that he has found it. Indeed, there are parallels between the character of Anakin Skywalker and Barack Obama. Both are born under mysterious circumstances to humble beginnings, and much was made of the messianic potential. Both were described as a "chosen one," in Obama's case either to gently mock the hyperbolic excesses of his campaign, or, as by his more extreme detractors, to equate him with the anti-Christ figure of the *Left Behind* series of evangelical apocalyptic novels. The former critique was more justified, as the press fawned over Obama, and heralded his election as the ushering in of a new "post-racial" utopia. Obama's own campaign rhetoric intruded on the Biblical, as he described his success as the "moment when the oceans ceased to rise."

But dictator Obama remains. Lest one think I am engaged in equally grandiose hyperbole, understand that I am being quite precise in my definition of dictator. Obama is not a dictator for life, but nor were the ancient Greek tyrants from which we get the term. As of this writing, Obama has not rejected, but in fact has reaffirmed the dictatorial powers of the presidency assumed by the Bush and Cheney administration. Specifically, he retains the power by dictat to declare American citizens enemy combatants, assassinate them, or thrown them in an oubliette as dark and inaccessible as any maintained by the absolute monarchs of pre-revolutionary France. His rejection of the right of habeas corpus, the foundation of Western liberty, and his re-affirmation of warrantless searches, contrary to the Fourth Amendment, place him securely in the ranks of dictators. Whether he is benevolent of not depends on ones' position. He is of little threat to Lucas and other wealthy elites, but it is unlikely that the citizens of Afghanistan or Iraq consider him benevolent. As of this writing, American citizens convicted of no crime remain imprisoned indefinitely by their own government, assumed guilty and with no recourse to prove their innocence. Obama is waging overt wars against Iraq and Afghanistan, a low-level intrusions into Pakistan and Somalia, and covert warfare against Iran. Obama has asserted and exercised an authority to assassinate any American citiizen he chooses merely at his own diktat. Cheney's Death Star remains "fully operational."

This illustrates the problem with Lucas' anti-democratic elitism and trust in an Übermensch, as well as his denial of absolute truth or morality. A rigorous application of an absolutist morality, such as just war theory, for example, would condemn both Bush and Obama equally for the wars that, presumably, Lucas was opposed to. Obama bears guilt for these in that as Senator he voted to fund these wars, as well as for his continuation, and in the case of Afghanistan, escalation, as President.

But if, as Lucas asserts in the prequels, there is no absolute standard of morality, and the actions of the elites are beyond the ken of the unwashed masses, then one can rest assured in the superficial changing of the guard. A "kinder and gentler " empire, led by the "Chosen One" can continue business as usual, but we can delude ourselves into thinking significant change was made, for only the Sith deal in absolutes.

Conclusion

The Original Star Wars trilogy was both artistically satisfying and ethically enriching because they encouraged us, through the Rick Blaine trope, to be better than ourselves, to join in a rebellion against evil, to withstand horrors and best them. The prequels failed both ethically and aesthetically, for they taught us to leave our trust in elites, to passively watch as they fight amongst themselves, and not to worry over much if the wrong guy wins, because there is no real good and evil anyway. This message, both nihilistic and elitist, was obscured for many by the adolescent spectacle of blasters, spaceships and lightsabers at war.

Perhaps the flash and bang of war blinded Lucas himself, for he has lost sight of his own wisdom, expressed through the words of Yoda in *The Empire Strikes Back,*

"Wars not make one great."

Appendix:
Don't Send In The Clones.

"All nations striving strong to make/red war yet redder.
Mad as hatters"
Thomas Hardy, *Channel Firing*

In his article *Send in the Clones: The Ethics of Future Wars* from the 2005 book *Star Wars and Philosophy,* Prof. Richard Hanley argues for the use of a cloned, slave army like the one used by the Jedi in *Attack of the Clones.* He is not merely arguing that it was ethical for the Jedi to create and use such soldiers in a galaxy far, far away, but that it could be ethical for just such an army to be created and used by humans, on Earth, in the near future.

His argument rests on two pillars. First, that the intentional cloning and genetic engineering of a population predisposed to obedience, and thus a natural slave 'race', can be justified under certain conditions. Second, that using such an enslaved population to wage war can also be justified under certain conditions.

For his first argument, he mercifully does not fall into the trap that some commentators on cloning have, that because they are cloned, and thus have identical genetic material to others, that they are somehow less than human, or not deserving of full human rights. A clone is no less a human being than a monozygotic twin is.

Indeed, the cloning is merely the most efficient

way to provide a universal, mass production template to facilitate the genetic engineering that is Hanley's goal. What Hanley desires to be engineered into these warriors is a compliant obedience to authority, as demonstrated by the clones in the Lucas' prequels. (However, the desire for such obedience in soldiers predates *Star Wars,* of course, and has been the dream of authority figures from Hassan-i Sabbah's legendary religion-and -hashish-addled assassins of the Eleventh Century to the United States' military and CIA Cold War experiments with mind control in the Twentieth Century.)

Hanley is arguing for just such a "diminished autonomy" to be engineered into the clone army. This is similar to the animal in Douglas Adams' science fiction classic *Restaurant at the End of the Universe,* which has been engineered to wish to be eaten. Hanley's clones would be similarly humorous- soldiers who wish to be drafted, to kill and be killed- if he were not seriously arguing for their creation.

His first justification of creating a slave race rests on the idea that creation of life is a good thing, and thus, as long as the negatives of that life- in this case, elimination of free will and compulsory military service, including the concomitant killing and risk of being killed, - are compensated with a sufficient level of positives, - presumably a decent standard of living, certain entertainments and pleasures, etc, to make the clone's life worth living,- then the creation of such a clone, in terms of the pain and pleasure suffered by the clone itself, is justified.

This is an expression of the simplest application of a form of ethical philosophy known as ethical utilitarianism. Advocated by Jeremy Bentham, John Stuart Mill and others, it argues that the ethical worth of actions can be evaluated by comparing the pleasure generated by the action (measured in the theoretical units of pleasure, "hedons") to the pain generated (measured in "dolors.") This is the thinking behind voting for the "lesser evil", for example. The logical, even mathematical precision of this theory of ethics has proven attractive to many in science fiction and is reflected in the Vulcan ethic of "The needs of the many outweigh the needs of the few."

However, since the initial development of this theory in the Eighteenth century, more sophisticated versions have been developed which evaluate ethical actions not so much on simple physical pleasure and pain, (criticized as the "pigs' philosphy") but on comparative levels of freedom, justice, human rights or dignity created by any given moral act. The basest interpretation of utilitarianism, that makes no allowance for the rights or consent of the subjects, could indeed be used to justify slavery, at least mild forms of it. (Another science fiction writer, the great Ursula K. LeGuin, critiqued just such a simplistic application in her classic short story, *The Ones Who Walk Away From Omelas.*)

Hanley does not detail how the lives of such soldiers could be constructed such that they would derive more pleasure than pain from a life of involuntary military service, in which a significant part of their lives are spent killing and facing the dangers of being killed or maimed in combat. Do they spend their downtime receiving pleasures, either in real life, or in some form of virtual reality? Are their memories of the horrors of warfare to be erased from their minds after each battle? Or, perhaps they have been engineered and programmed to derive pleasure from killing? That would seem to be the most efficient way of resolving the problem- that is, creating an army of psychopaths. The mind recoils.

Having resolved to his satisfaction that the creation of clone soldiers is not inherently unethical, Hanley then seeks to justify their deployment by recourse to Just War Theory. This ethical theory has its origins in the Roman Catholic Church and such Church Fathers as St. Augustine of Hippo and St. Thomas Aquinas. However, the theory is not at its core built on a scriptural foundation, and one does not have to be religious at all to apply it. Instead, Just War Theory is based on the premise that one human life is as entitled to protection as any other and thus is truly "catholic" in the sense of universal.

The origins of Just War Theory are found in the historically anomalous situation that after the fall of the Roman Empire in Europe, the Catholic Church had some degree of moral authority over several separate and often warring states. Thus, unlike many historical situations in which a church is coterminous with a state, and therefore the priests simply give their carte blanche blessing to the warriors of one nation to kill those of another, the Catholic Church could not, for example, declare the lives of Frenchmen to be less valid than those of Spaniards.

Instead, all of Just War theory follows logically from the premise that one life is as valid as any other. From this premise several principles are derived, such as proportionality- that is, that even if a war is fought for a just cause, that is, to prevent a harm, the force used and damage done must not exceed the potential harm that is trying to be prevented. Space precludes a thorough discussion of all of the elements of Just War Theory here, but if a war meets all of the criteria for a Just War such that it has a reasonable chance of preventing a greater harm while protecting civilians, it is immoral to *not* fight such a war, (assuming for the moment that one is not an absolute pacifist.) Hanley assumes that his clone army would be employed in such a war, though he does concede that such opportunities might be rare.

Here is the greatest weakness in Hanley's argument- he supports the creation of a slave army to fight just wars, and ignores their role in *unjust* wars. While one might be tempted to dismiss all unjust wars as equally invalid, a more detailed analysis is warranted. First, if we leave the galaxy of Star Wars, and look at wars as they are fought on Earth, a rigorous application of Just War theory reveals that Just Wars, that are fought both for just reasons and using just methods are so rare as to be practically non-existent. (As both my nationality and expertise are American, I will confine my discussion to US wars, but I am confident that an application of Just War Theory to other conflicts would yield similar results.) Even the presumed "Good War" of World War II does not meet the criteria for a just war. There was a potential for a just cause in going to war (*Jus ad bellum)* in protecting the Jews and others from the Nazi Holocaust. However, America did not enter the war for that reason, and the US even turned back a boat of Jewish refugees, the *MS St. Louis* in 1939.

Further, when conducting the war, the United States committed numerous violations of the standards for just wartime conduct (*Jus in bello)* ranging from the internment of its own Japanese citizens, to the use of weapons of mass destruction on civilian populations at Hiroshima and Nagasaki.

A thorough examination of the historical record suggest that if such a clone army were created, it would be far more likely to be used in an unjust war than in a just one. However, one might claim that such deployment would not necessarily make such wars worse. Such an argument fails under close examination, as a clone army would have great potential to make unjust wars *more* unjust.

How does one prevent or deter unjust wars? The nations of the world have signed the Geneva Conventions and other treaties that prohibit unjust wars, but the enforcement of these has been spotty at best and is often a case of "victor's justice." One might hope that the decision makers – both politicians, and in democracies, the populace- that send troops to battle and order their conduct might voluntarily adhere to such standards as matters of conscience. Yet the historical record suggests, at best, indifference to these concerns on the part of the American electorate and those they elect.

Yet there is one area of resistance to unjust wars- disobedience of the part of the soldiery and those who might be drafted into their ranks. Indeed, the Nuremberg Principles codified after World War II mandate such disobedience to unjust orders. "I was just following orders" is not a valid defense when accused of war crimes.

The infamous massacre at My Lai during the Vietnam War is an instructive example. While many may have a vague awareness of this incident in which hundreds of innocent Vietnamese civilians were slaughtered by American troops. Because this is the only such incident many Americans are aware of, they may think it was an aberration. My Lai was unusual, but not for being a massacre. Such massacres were commonplace in Vietnam and consistent with the US military's policy and objectives, but what distinguished My Lai from the others was that Hugh Thompson, the pilot of one of the helicopters involved intervened on behalf of the innocent civilians. Thompson not only evacuated Vietnamese away from the killing field, but ordered his door gunner to fire on their own troops if necessary to protect the civilians.

Nor was Thompson alone in such resistance. In Vietnam soldiers and sailors mutinied, deserted, committed acts of sabotage, and refused orders to resist the unjust war. Others resisted the war by avoiding the draft and military service altogether.

In his famous studies of conformity in the 1960s, the social psychologist Stanley Milgram discovered that 65% of Americans would administer what they believed were fatal electric shocks to another person if a man in a white lab coat told them to. Horrific as that may be, one can take comfort in the knowledge that at some point nearly half of the test subjects said no and refused.

If we were to "send in the clones" as Prof. Hanley argues, we would lose that percentage of people that would disobey unjust orders. There are no Hugh Thompsons in an army of cloned slaves engineered to obey orders with "diminished autonomy." A clone army is most likely to be employed in an unjust war, and will make such a war more unjust.

Nor is this merely an academic exercise. While genetically engineered clone slave armies may be a few decades off, the US military is currently working to improve the artificial intelligence of their drones such that they can follow their own programming in deciding to kill, thus removing the conscience of a human operator from the process. Indeed, this appendix can be re-read with the word "drone" substituted for "clone" and the argument still stands.

Whether flesh or steel, genetically or electronically engineered, an army of merciless killers, incapable of saying "no" to even the most atrocious orders, is to be greatly feared, and is no longer only to be found in the confines of science fiction. Mad as hatters, indeed.

www.ingramcontent.com/pod-product-compliance
Ingram Content Group UK Ltd.
Pitfield, Milton Keynes, MK11 3LW, UK
UKHW020221250726
13967UKWH00001B/129

9 781300 456766